T0311403

An Analysis of

David C. Kang's

China Rising
Peace, Power, and Order
in East Asia

Matteo Dian
with
Jason Xidias

Published by Macat International Ltd
24:13 Coda Centre, 189 Munster Road, London SW6 6AW.

Distributed exclusively by Routledge
2 Park Square, Milton Park, Abingdon, Oxon OX14 4RN
711 Third Avenue, New York, NY 10017, USA

Routledge is an imprint of the Taylor & Francis Group, an informa business

Copyright © 2017 by Macat International Ltd
Macat International has asserted its right under the Copyright, Designs and Patents Act
1988 to be identified as the copyright holder of this work.

The print publication is protected by copyright. Prior to any prohibited reproduction, storage in
a retrieval system, distribution or transmission in any form or by any means, electronic, mechanical, recording or otherwise, permission should be obtained from the publisher or where
applicable a license permitting restricted copying in the United Kingdom should be obtained
from the Copyright Licensing Agency Ltd, Barnard's Inn, 86 Fetter Lane, London EC4A 1EN, UK.

The ePublication is protected by copyright and must not be copied, reproduced, transferred,
distributed, leased, licensed or publicly performed or used in any way except as specifically
permitted in writing by the publishers, as allowed under the terms and conditions under which
it was purchased, or as strictly permitted by applicable copyright law. Any unauthorised distribution or use of this text may be a direct infringement of the authors and the publishers' rights
and those responsible may be liable in law accordingly.

www.macat.com
info@macat.com

Cataloguing in Publication Data
A catalogue record for this book is available from the British Library.
Library of Congress Cataloguing-in-Publication Data is available upon request.
Cover illustration: Etienne Gilfillan

ISBN 978-1-912303-31-1 (hardback)
ISBN 978-1-912128-96-9 (paperback)
ISBN 978-1-912282-19-7 (e-book)

Notice
The information in this book is designed to orientate readers of the work under analysis,
to elucidate and contextualise its key ideas and themes, and to aid in the development
of critical thinking skills. It is not meant to be used, nor should it be used, as a
substitute for original thinking or in place of original writing or research. References and
notes are provided for informational purposes and their presence does not constitute
endorsement of the information or opinions therein. This book is presented solely for
educational purposes. It is sold on the understanding that the publisher is not engaged
to provide any scholarly advice. The publisher has made every effort to ensure that
this book is accurate and up-to-date, but makes no warranties or representations with
regard to the completeness or reliability of the information it contains. The information
and the opinions provided herein are not guaranteed or warranted to produce particular
results and may not be suitable for students of every ability. The publisher shall not be
liable for any loss, damage or disruption arising from any errors or omissions, or from
the use of this book, including, but not limited to, special, incidental, consequential or
other damages caused, or alleged to have been caused, directly or indirectly, by the
information contained within.

CONTENTS

WAYS IN TO THE TEXT

Who Is David C. Kang?   9

What Does *China Rising* Say?   10

Why Does *China Rising* Matter?   12

SECTION 1: INFLUENCES

Module 1: The Author and the Historical Context   15

Module 2: Academic Context   19

Module 3: The Problem   24

Module 4: The Author's Contribution   28

SECTION 2: IDEAS

Module 5: Main Ideas   34

Module 6: Secondary Ideas   38

Module 7: Achievement   44

Module 8: Place in the Author's Work   48

SECTION 3: IMPACT

Module 9: The First Responses   53

Module 10: The Evolving Debate   58

Module 11: Impact and Influence Today   62

Module 12: Where Next?   67

Glossary of Terms   73

People Mentioned in the Text   79

Works Cited   84

THE MACAT LIBRARY

The Macat Library is a series of unique academic explorations of seminal works in the humanities and social sciences – books and papers that have had a significant and widely recognised impact on their disciplines. It has been created to serve as much more than just a summary of what lies between the covers of a great book. It illuminates and explores the influences on, ideas of, and impact of that book. Our goal is to offer a learning resource that encourages critical thinking and fosters a better, deeper understanding of important ideas.

Each publication is divided into three Sections: Influences, Ideas, and Impact. Each Section has four Modules. These explore every important facet of the work, and the responses to it.

This Section-Module structure makes a Macat Library book easy to use, but it has another important feature. Because each Macat book is written to the same format, it is possible (and encouraged!) to cross-reference multiple Macat books along the same lines of inquiry or research. This allows the reader to open up interesting interdisciplinary pathways.

To further aid your reading, lists of glossary terms and people mentioned are included at the end of this book (these are indicated by an asterisk [*] throughout) – as well as a list of works cited.

Macat has worked with the University of Cambridge to identify the elements of critical thinking and understand the ways in which six different skills combine to enable effective thinking.
Three allow us to fully understand a problem; three more give us the tools to solve it. Together, these six skills make up the **PACIER** model of critical thinking. They are:

ANALYSIS – understanding how an argument is built
EVALUATION – exploring the strengths and weaknesses of an argument
INTERPRETATION – understanding issues of meaning

CREATIVE THINKING – coming up with new ideas and fresh connections
PROBLEM-SOLVING – producing strong solutions
REASONING – creating strong arguments

To find out more, visit **WWW.MACAT.COM.**

CRITICAL THINKING AND *CHINA RISING*

Primary critical thinking skill: CREATIVE THINKING
Secondary critical thinking skill: EVALUATION

David C. Kang's *China Rising* is a fine example of an author making use of creative thinking skills to reach a conclusion that flies in the face of traditional thinking.

The conventional view that the book opposed, known in international relations as 'realism,' was that the rise of any new global power results in global or regional instability. As such, China's development as a world economic powerhouse worried mainstream western geopolitical scholars, whose concerns were based on the realist assumption that individual countries will inevitably compete for dominance. Evaluating these arguments, and finding both their relevance and adequacy wanting, Kang instead turned traditional thinking on its head by looking at Asian history without preconceptions, and with analytical open-mindedness.

Producing several novel explanations for existing evidence, Kang concludes that China's neighbors do not want to compete with it in the way that realist interpretations predict. Rather than creating instability by jockeying for position, he argues, surrounding countries are happy for China to be acknowledged as a leader, believing that its dominant position will stabilize Asia, and give the whole region more of a hand in international relations.

Though critics have taken issue with Kang's conclusions, his paradigm-shifting approach is nevertheless an excellent example of developing fresh new conclusions through creative thinking.

ABOUT THE AUTHOR OF THE ORIGINAL WORK

Born in 1965, **David C. Kang** is a political scientist specializing in East Asia, and China and Korea in particular. He was raised in California, the son of early-wave Korean immigrants, and– having previously been a visiting professor at universities in the United States, Europe, and Asia–is currently professor of international relations and business, and director of the Korean Studies Institute, at the University of Southern California. Kang has authored four books, and has published numerous scholarly and popular articles. His collaborations with colleagues who have fundamentally opposing views, such as his dialogue with political scientist Victor Cha, demonstrate his commitment to conversation and cooperation across ideological divides.

ABOUT THE AUTHORS OF THE ANALYSIS

Dr Matteo Dian holds a PhD in international relations from the Scuola Normale Superiore di Pisa, where he research focused on the evolution of the US-Japanese alliance after World War II. He is currently a research fellow at the University of Bologna, where he continues to work on international relations with a special focus on the place of China in world politics.

Dr Jason Xidias holds a PhD in European Politics from King's College London, where he completed a comparative dissertation on immigration and citizenship in Britain and France. He was also a Visiting Fellow in European Politics at the University of California, Berkeley. Currently, he is Lecturer in Political Science at New York University.

ABOUT MACAT

GREAT WORKS FOR CRITICAL THINKING

Macat is focused on making the ideas of the world's great thinkers accessible and comprehensible to everybody, everywhere, in ways that promote the development of enhanced critical thinking skills.

It works with leading academics from the world's top universities to produce new analyses that focus on the ideas and the impact of the most influential works ever written across a wide variety of academic disciplines. Each of the works that sit at the heart of its growing library is an enduring example of great thinking. But by setting them in context – and looking at the influences that shaped their authors, as well as the responses they provoked – Macat encourages readers to look at these classics and game-changers with fresh eyes. Readers learn to think, engage and challenge their ideas, rather than simply accepting them.

'Macat offers an amazing first-of-its-kind tool for interdisciplinary learning and research. Its focus on works that transformed their disciplines and its rigorous approach, drawing on the world's leading experts and educational institutions, opens up a world-class education to anyone.'

Andreas Schleicher
Director for Education and Skills, Organisation for Economic
Co-operation and Development

'Macat is taking on some of the major challenges in university education … They have drawn together a strong team of active academics who are producing teaching materials that are novel in the breadth of their approach.'

Prof Lord Broers,
former Vice-Chancellor of the University of Cambridge

'The Macat vision is exceptionally exciting. It focuses upon new modes of learning which analyse and explain seminal texts which have profoundly influenced world thinking and so social and economic development. It promotes the kind of critical thinking which is essential for any society and economy.
This is the learning of the future.'

Rt Hon Charles Clarke, former UK Secretary of State for Education

'The Macat analyses provide immediate access to the critical conversation surrounding the books that have shaped their respective discipline, which will make them an invaluable resource to all of those, students and teachers, working in the field.'

Professor William Tronzo, University of California at San Diego

WAYS IN TO THE TEXT

KEY POINTS

- David C. Kang (b. 1965) is an American political scientist specializing in East Asia, especially China and Korea.

- He argues that as a result of shared Asian history and identity, neighboring countries see China's ascent as natural and legitimate, and essential for peace and stability in the region.

- *China Rising* links particularities of Asian history and identity to international relations theory—theoretical explanations of the interactions between nation states*— to argue that China's increasing global influence is a positive development.

Who Is David C. Kang?

David C. Kang, the author of *China Rising: Peace, Power, and Order in East Asia* (2007), is an American political scientist specializing in East Asia, with a particular focus on China and Korea. Son of Korean immigrants, he grew up in California, and embarked on an impressive academic career, receiving his BA in anthropology and international relations from Stanford University in 1988, and his MA and PhD in political science from the University of California at Berkeley in 1995. From 1996 to 2007, he taught government and business at Dartmouth College in New Hampshire, and since 2009 he has been professor of international relations and business at the University of Southern California. At USC, he is also the director of the Korean Studies Institute. He has been a visiting professor at Seoul National University, Korea University, the University of Geneva, Yale University, and the University of California, San Diego.

Kang has built his reputation through his innovative research into economic development, security, and the historical basis of contemporary international relations. At the time of writing, he has authored four books, edited one, and published numerous articles in academic journals, including *International Organization*, *International Security*, and the *European Journal of International Relations*. His latest book is *East Asia before the West: Five Centuries of Trade and Tribute* (2010).

Kang also reaches a general audience beyond the academic world as a frequent contributor to the popular press, with opinion pieces on the foreign affairs of the United States, South Korea, North Korea, China, and Japan published in the *New York Times*, the *Financial Times*, the *Washington Post*, and the *Los Angeles Times*, in addition to a monthly column in Korean for the *Joongang Ilbo* (*Central Times*).

Finally, Kang is on numerous academic editorial boards, including *Pacific Affairs*, *Political Science Quarterly*, and *Political Research Quarterly*.

What Does *China Rising* Say?

China Rising presents two main arguments. It begins by proposing a theoretical alternative to realism*—a school of thought in the field of international relations that argues individual countries are the primary actors in international affairs, and they seek to maximize their power and security against other states in an environment where there is no effective presiding global authority or world government body.

In contrast to realist theory, Kang argues that national and regional identity is key for understanding the relations between countries. Drawing from the German political scientist Alexander Wendt's* *Social Theory of International Politics*, Kang claims that states have a relatively stable understanding of themselves and others.[1] This influences their perception of the outside world, and determines whether they consider other states to be potential partners or adversaries, and whether they support the rise and leadership of one major power in a region (in this case, China).

This theoretical position leads to Kang's second main argument: that East Asian countries have largely welcomed China's ascent toward superpower status. Kang attributes this to two factors. First, China's rise helps all East Asian nations to grow economically; second, East Asian countries consider China's regional leadership as legitimate because of their shared history and identity—a "Sinocentric"* view, acknowledging China's long history of regional dominance. The prevailing view is that an economically and militarily strong China has never been a source of instability or conflict; on the contrary, the Asian continent has suffered greater instability and war when China has been weak, as was the case, for example, during the period between the end of the nineteenth and the beginning of the twentieth centuries.

Most East Asian states define their identity in relation to the Sinocentric system—a kind of regional hierarchy* operating between 1300 and 1900 within which China, holding the superior position, received tributes from other states. China was at the center of an integrated international system in which trade, which it promoted, flourished, and in which war between Asian states was rare; it did not attempt to conquer its neighbors by military force. As a result, Kang shows, East Asian nations never sought to form an alliance to balance, contain, or oppose China's power.

East Asian states considered the Sinocentric system both legitimate and advantageous in terms of stability and economic growth. Therefore, according to Kang, they do not fear the economic and military rise China has enjoyed since 1979. Instead, they see it as China's natural return to leadership and an essential engine of regional development.

China Rising is an original contribution to international relations, making a novel connection between international relations theory and interstate politics in Asia. Kang presents a clear understanding of China's rise and leadership in Asia, and argues that we must see this as a positive and stabilizing development. Furthermore, he advises the United States and other powers such as Japan and South Korea to avoid conflict and to cooperate with China. This, he argues, is the best strategy if greater economic growth and global peace are to be achieved.

Why Does *China Rising* Matter?

Since 1991, the close of the long period of global nuclear tension that defined the Cold War,* American presidential administrations have struggled to find the right mix of engagement and confrontation with China. While the administration of President Bill Clinton* (1993–2001) worked toward including China in the World Trade Organization (WTO),* a global institution based in Switzerland that addresses the rules of international trade, it also confronted China, even threatening force during the Taiwan Strait Crisis* in 1996 (a series of conflicts between China and Taiwan over disputed territory).[2] The administration of George W. Bush* (2001–9) adopted a similarly mixed approach, encouraging commercial cooperation while pressuring China to reform its policies in several areas, including human rights;[3] while the administration of Barack Obama* (2009–16) initially seemed favorable to a policy of engagement and partnership, it soon shifted toward a more competitive, confrontational approach, seeking to expand its commercial and military ties with other Asian states.[4]

China Rising is a timely attempt to frame China's ascent as an opportunity rather than a threat for the United States, and for the West more broadly. The text speaks to academics, policy-makers, and readers with a general interest in current international relations. Kang puts forward a credible alternative to the image of China as a revisionist power*—a state that aggressively seeks to alter the international order. He advances a comprehensive and well-articulated argument in favor of the inclusion of China as a productive partner within the present economic and political global order, claiming that this will bring about greater global peace and stability.

The core of Kang's argument is that America's attempt to use its influence in the Asian region to contain China's ascent through things such as alliances, and so on, has the potential to create serious instability, and compel Asian states to choose between Washington and Beijing, rather than being strong partners of both.

On the other hand, if America, and other major powers, cooperate with China and seek to better integrate it into the existing international order, this could prevent it from being aggressive, and consequently ensure greater political and economic stability for all. Even in making this argument, Kang shows that he also understands the fear of many policy-makers in Washington that an unchallenged China could undermine American power, influence, and security both in the East Asian region and globally.

NOTES

1   Alexander Wendt, *Social Theory of International Politics* (Cambridge: Cambridge University Press, 1999).

2   Ramon H. Myers, Michael Oksenberg, and David Shambaugh, *Making China Policy: Lessons from the Bush and Clinton Administrations* (Lanham, MD: Rowman & Littlefield, 2001); Robert S. Ross, "The 1995–96 Taiwan Strait Confrontation: Coercion, Credibility, and the Use of Force," *International Security* 25, no. 2 (2000): 87–123.

3   David Shambaugh, "Coping with a Conflicted China," *The Washington Quarterly* 34, no. 1 (2011): 7–27.

4   Daniel Drezner, "Does Obama Have a Grand Strategy? Why We Need Doctrines in Uncertain Times," *Foreign Affairs* 90, no. 4 (2011): 57–62.

SECTION 1
INFLUENCES

MODULE 1
THE AUTHOR AND THE
HISTORICAL CONTEXT

KEY POINTS

- *China Rising* is an important contribution to academic and political debates on the rise of China and its consequences for international relations.

- David C. Kang is a well-known political scientist specializing in East Asia, especially China and Korea.

- Since the end of the nuclear standoff between the Soviet Union* and the United States known as the Cold War* in 1991, American presidential administrations have struggled to formulate a consistent foreign policy toward China.

Why Read This Text?

David C. Kang's *China Rising* (2007) makes an important contribution to the theory and practice of contemporary international relations.

Kang fuses liberal* and constructivist* principles to challenge the dominant realist* position in the discipline: according to the liberal approach in international relations, cooperation, trade, and economic interdependence* reduce the risk of war; according to constructivist thought, states behave in line with their perception of themselves and other states, which they may consider as friends, rivals, or enemies. His approach, then, highlights the role that economic ties play in building peace, security, and prosperity, and emphasizes the importance of shared history and identity in pan-Asian decision-making.

The author stresses how a long history of common ideas and identity in Asia has informed a majority understanding among Asian

> ❝ China's expected emergence as the most powerful
> state in East Asia has been accompanied with more
> stability than pessimists believed because China is
> increasingly becoming the regional hierarch. On the
> one hand, China has provided credible information
> about its capabilities and intentions to its neighbors. On
> the other hand, East Asian states actually believe China's
> claims, and hence do not fear—and instead seek to
> benefit from—China's rise. ❞
>
> David C. Kang, "Why China's Rise Will Be Peaceful: Hierarchy and Stability
> in the East Asian Region"

nations that China's rise is natural, legitimate, and most of all beneficial
for regional stability and prosperity.

Kang goes on to argue that established European theories of
international relations may not be the best fit for studying the specific
nature of historical and contemporary developments in Asian
international relations. Shaking up some of the dominant assumptions
in his field, he provides a fresh analytical framework and interpretation,
and encourages even more novel, non-Western approaches in the
discipline.

Finally, he contributes to ongoing political debates about the rise
of China and its consequences for international relations in the United
States and elsewhere. In doing so, he challenges the mainstream
perspective that China's ascent poses a threat to the West. As Kang sees
it, China's strength will lead to greater regional and global peace and
stability if the United States and its allies help facilitate this
development rather than attempt to confront or contain it.

The emergence of China as a major player on the international
stage is one of the most significant developments in contemporary
geopolitics. Kang's call for understanding and engagement over

containment*—using alliances to try to prevent a great power's growth—and confrontation make *China Rising* a must-read for those who are interested in international politics, particularly Asian and Chinese–American foreign relations.

Author's Life

David C. Kang was born in 1965 to Korean immigrant parents, and grew up in California. He gained his BA in anthropology and international relations at Stanford University, and then completed an MA and a PhD in political science at the University of California, Berkeley. After his studies, he took up an academic appointment at Dartmouth College in government and business, and then moved on to the University of Southern California, where he is currently professor of international relations and business, and director of the Korean Studies Institute.

Kang is widely regarded as an eminent expert on East Asia, and in particular on China and Korea. He has written four books: *Crony Capitalism: Corruption and Development in South Korea and the Philippines* (2002), *Nuclear North Korea: A Debate on Engagement Strategies* (2003), *China Rising: Peace, Power, and Order in East Asia* (2007), and *East Asia before the West: Five Centuries of Trade and Tribute* (2010), as well as editing another titled *Engagement with North Korea: A Viable Alternative* (2009). He has also authored more than 20 articles in respected academic journals. His main areas of research are economic development, security, and the historical basis of contemporary international relations.

Author's Background

David C. Kang's *China Rising* addresses one of the most important academic and political debates in international relations today: China's economic and military rise, its potential consequences, and how the rest of the world should approach it.

17

Kang starts with the basics of the contemporary situation: the United States and China are currently the two largest economies in the world, China is the biggest foreign creditor of the United States, and the two countries share important political and security interests, including preventing terrorism and the spread of nuclear weapons; meanwhile, there are many points of tension between the two countries over issues such as democracy and human rights, Taiwan, and China's extension of power and influence in Asia. This mixed bag of interests leads the United States and China to see themselves as both allies and adversaries.

China Rising details the complex history of relations between China and the United States since 1945, dedicating most of its focus to the changes in relations between the two countries since 1979, and especially since the end of the Cold War. Formal diplomatic relations between the two states were established in 1979. Since the collapse of the Soviet Union—the United States' primary global rival—in 1991, China's rise has been a subject of increasing prominence in academic and political debates. These have focused on two possibilities: one is that China could be reformed democratically and integrated into the world economy; the other is that China could use its newfound wealth to bolster its military might, intimidate its neighbors, threaten American interests in Asia, and destabilize the Western-led international order.

In *China Rising*, David C. Kang presents a detailed historical analysis, grounded in international relations theory, that defends the former perspective. In doing so, he advises the United States and its Asian allies to cooperate with China rather than try to confront or contain it.

MODULE 2
ACADEMIC CONTEXT

KEY POINTS

- In *China Rising*, David C. Kang makes an important contribution to academic and political debates regarding China, Chinese–American relations, and East Asian international relations.

- Realism* is the belief that international relations exist in an anarchic* (ungoverned) environment and that conflict is largely unavoidable; Kang presents a coherent alternative to the realist view that the United States should confront China because it represents a threat to American and East Asian power and security.

- Since publication in 2007, *China Rising* has been a key reference point for academics and policy-makers who see the potential benefits of China's strength and prominence.

The Work in Its Context

David C. Kang's analytical framework in *China Rising* draws on three theories in international relations: realism, liberalism,* and constructivism.*

Realists argue that states react to the ascent of a new great power by seeking to balance its power. This can occur through internal balancing (increasing their own military capabilities), or through external balancing (forming new alliances with other states). Realists use the term "bandwagoning"* to refer to a weaker state aligning with a stronger state, or with a state that represents a threat to its security.

The realist stance is essentially pessimistic about human nature. It argues that international politics are inherently competitive, and states, who are the main actors in international affairs, seek to maintain or

> **❝** China's behavior during the Ming Dynasty was consistent with the predictions of realism; then, as now, China behaved no differently than any rising power would have done. For some, this is a cause for celebration; for others, fear. **❞**
>
> Vinod K. Aggarwal and Sara A. Newland, "Introduction," in *Responding to China's Rise: US and EU Strategies*

expand their power and security in a state of anarchy: there is no single higher authority or world government effectively managing relations between states.

Liberal theories of international relations argue that several factors can contribute to stabilizing international politics and making conflict less likely, such as trade and economic interdependence,* and the spread of democracy. Liberals also recognize that international institutions play an important role in encouraging cooperation and maintaining peace and stability.

Constructivism argues that while the pursuit of power and security is an important factor, states' behavior is primarily driven by their identities and ideas. In other words, states act according to their perception of themselves and other states, which they may consider as friends, rivals, or enemies. These ideas form and develop through social interaction across time.

In *China Rising*, Kang challenges the realist approach, while fusing liberalism and constructivism to build his core argument.

Overview of the Field

The intellectual environment that Kang operates in influences his work in two main ways. First, he uses an established theoretical framework, taken from realist, liberal, and constructivist approaches to international relations theory. Concepts such as hierarchy,* economic interdependence, balance of power,* and bandwagoning are long-standing foundations of theories generated in the discipline.

Second, Kang builds his argument by considering the reaction of other Asian countries to China's increasing global influence. As he observes, China's rise has been accepted by other Asian states due to the political and cultural legacy of the region's "Sinocentric system,"* which assumes the political superiority of the Chinese state. This approach owes a debt to the work of the thinkers John K. Fairbank* and Ta-Tuan Ch'en,* who helped establish Asian Studies as an academic discipline and who first proposed this perspective in the 1940s. Before Western colonization, they argue, Asian international relations were characterized by a hierarchical system in which China was considered superior to other states in the region; recognizing this Sinocentric system is the key to understanding international relations in Asia.[1]

The value of Kang's work lies in the power of his empirical analysis (that is, an analysis based on evidence verifiable by observation), rooted in a solid theoretical framework, enabling him to explain long-term trends and also prescribe solutions for American and Asian policymakers. Combining liberalism and constructivism, he promotes a convincing alternative to the realist assessment of the Chinese rise that has been dominant both in academic and political debates. His argument that accommodating China's rise can provide greater regional and global peace and stability has attracted considerable attention.

Academic Influences

A desire to shake up the dominance of realist theory in international relations influenced both Kang's theoretical approach and his choice of research themes. His first theoretical sparring partners were his colleagues at the University of California, Berkeley, where he received his Master's degree and PhD. These include Kenneth N. Waltz,* a

Berkeley professor who formulated the balance of power theory (according to which nations take action, such as forming alliances, to limit the disproportional power of a single state), and Stephen Walt,* a former Berkeley PhD student, who developed the main variant of the balance of power theory: the balance of threat theory.* The essential difference between these two approaches lies in the claim that states do not balance against power but against a *threat*: a nearby state that possesses both substantial military capabilities *and* the willingness to use them.

Kang draws a direct link between his Korean heritage and his perspective on international relations in the preface of his later book *East Asia before the West: Five Centuries of Trade and Tribute* (2010).[2] He sees international relations theory as excessively modeled on European and Western history, and therefore largely unable to grasp the cultural and historical peculiarities of Asia. Instead, Kang continues in the footsteps of John K. Fairbank, one of the first scholars to theorize Asian relations in terms of the Sinocentric order, which recognizes China as a natural and legitimate leader of East Asia.

Since the Sinocentric order was hierarchical, it could not be analyzed employing the realist approach, according to which countries are seen as not only inherently competitive but also as broadly equal players without an overriding global body governing them. Realism cannot accommodate the possibility that states might recognize and accept as legitimate the superior position of another state. Consequently, in *China Rising*, Kang combines Fairbank's insight with a mixed methodology approach defined as analytical eclecticism* (that is, its analytical method draws on several different theories).[3] This approach allows him to test his main hypothesis: that Asian states have welcomed China's rise, thinking China is returning to occupy the same central role it had between the fourteenth and nineteenth centuries.

NOTES

1   John King Fairbank and *Ta-tuan Ch'en,* The Chinese World Order: Traditional China's Foreign Relations (Cambridge, MA: Harvard University Press, 1968).

2   David C. Kang, *East Asia before the West: Five Centuries of Trade and Tribute* (New York: Columbia University Press, 2010), 4.

3   Rudra Sil and Peter Katzenstein, "Analytic Eclecticism in the Study of World Politics: Reconfiguring Problems and Mechanisms across Research Traditions," *Perspectives on Politics* 8, no. 2 (2010): 411–31.

MODULE 3
THE PROBLEM

KEY POINTS

- In *China Rising*, David C. Kang analyzes China's rise, and the consequences of this rise for international relations.

- The author fuses liberal* and constructivist* theories of international relations to present an alternative to realism;* according to liberal theory, if nations cooperate, trade, and depend on each other economically, war will be avoided; according to constructivist theory, states behave according to their perception of themselves and the other states, which they may consider as friends, rivals, or enemies.

- Kang argues that Asian countries see Chinese leadership as natural and legitimate, and as an opportunity for greater political and economic leadership in the region. The West, therefore, should adopt a cooperative rather than confrontational stance toward China.

Core Question

David C. Kang's *China Rising* addresses one of the most relevant issues in academic and political debate: China's emergence as an economic and military superpower, and the consequences of this for international relations.

Kang asks whether China's rise will create instability and conflict in Asia, and ultimately undermine the current international order, or whether it will promote economic growth and a more stable international system. He argues that due to the economic and military might of China, this question is of the utmost relevance to the region and the world.

❝ China has silenced most of its critics by achieving near double-digit growth in the first decade of the 21st century. China has replaced Germany as the world's largest exporter and the third largest economy … Moreover, while American and European economies have been badly battered by the financial tsunami of 2008, the PRC [People's Republic of China] has been relatively unscathed and expected to recover first from the recession. **❞**

Herbert Yee, "Introduction," *China's Rise—Threat or Opportunity?*

The question fits a broader debate in international relations. Optimists, mainly inspired by liberal theories, argue that both Western and Asian countries should take full advantage of the opportunity offered by China's exceptional rise. Economically, China can be a major engine of future growth and development; politically, a more powerful China could help bring about a more plural global order. Consequently, both Western and Asian states should accommodate China's rise and build stronger relationships with it. Pessimists, in contrast, inspired by realist theories, tend to consider China's ascent as inherently dangerous in a world in which there is no world government regulating relations between states.[1] Left unchecked, a more powerful China could use its economic might and military power to pursue its national interests aggressively, threatening regional and global stability.

The Participants

From a theoretical perspective, Kang argues in favor of a viable alternative to realism in order to better explain East Asian international relations. He then proposes a framework inspired by liberal and constructivist approaches.

Advocates of liberalism argue that trade and economic interdependence* foster stability and diminish the likelihood of conflict, since all states who trade gain from it to a varying degree. Therefore, the rise of a great power is an opportunity for new commercial relations, greater economic growth, and stability.

Constructivists argue that ideas and identities are essential to understanding states' behavior. In other words, states will respond to the rise of a great power according to how they perceive themselves and their relationship with that state. Kang employs both liberal and constructivist principles to link Asian history and identities with current developments in international relations.

Kang combines these two theoretical approaches to contrast the realist view that, although states may cooperate at times, their primary goal is to maintain or increase their own power. Consequently, trade and interdependence do not render war obsolete or less likely. States see the rise of a great power as a threat to security more than an opportunity for economic growth.

The Contemporary Debate

Theoretical debates in international relations between realists, liberals, and constructivists are particularly prominent on the subject of the rise of China, and disputes over how the world should respond have been continuous since the 1990s. Several authors, mainly belonging to the realist school of thought, suggest that the ascent of a great power will necessarily lead to instability and conflict. Consequently, the United States should consider China a challenge to their global leadership and actively try to contain its rise. Key figures who have put forth this position include the political scientist Richard Betts* and the international relations theorist John Mearsheimer.*

Followers of liberal theory argue that China is not a threat for Asian countries or American leadership, highlighting the positive role China has played for Asian economic development, and how American and Chinese interests are indeed converging due to the high degree of financial and economic interdependence they have with each other.[2] China's entry into international institutions like the World Trade Organization (WTO),* an institution founded to promote international trade, serve as evidence to support the liberal view that China has begun to be successfully integrated into the Western global order and can rise peacefully to become a leading world power.[3]

Constructivist scholars place national and regional identity at the center of their interpretations and predictions.[4] Their acknowledgment of the conventions that have persisted through history and helped inform a shared Asian identity undermines the pessimism of the realist approach. In *China Rising*, Kang engages each of these approaches and through this engagement makes an important contribution to this debate.

NOTES

1   Richard K. Betts, "Wealth, Power, and Instability: East Asia and the United States after the Cold War," *International Security* 18, no. 3 (1993): 34–77; Aaron L. Friedberg, "Ripe for Rivalry: Prospects for Peace in a Multipolar Asia," *International Security* 18, no. 3 (1993): 5–33; John J. Mearsheimer, "China's Unpeaceful Rise," *Current History* 105, no. 690 (2006): 160–2.

2   James L. Richardson, "Asia-Pacific: The Case for Geopolitical Optimism," *National Interest*, 38 (1994): 28–39; Niall Ferguson and Moritz Schularick, "'Chimerica' and the Global Asset Market Boom," *International Finance* 10, no. 3 (2007): 215–39.

3   G. John Ikenberry, "The Rise of China and the Future of the West: Can the Liberal System Survive?" *Foreign Affairs* 87, no. 1 (2008): 23–37; Elizabeth C. Economy and Michel Oksenberg, eds., *China Joins the World: Progress and Prospects* (New York: Council on Foreign Relations, 1999); Marc Lanteigne, *China and International Institutions: Alternate Paths to Global Power* (Abingdon: Routledge, 2005).

4   Alastair Iain Johnston, "Is China a Status Quo Power?" International Security 27, no. 4 (2003): 5–56; Amitav Acharya, *Whose Ideas Matter? Agency and Power in Asian Regionalism* (Ithaca, NY: Cornell University Press, 2009).

MODULE 4
THE AUTHOR'S CONTRIBUTION

KEY POINTS

- In *China Rising*, David C. Kang challenges Eurocentric* interpretations of Asian international relations by detailing shared East Asian history and identity, and showing how perceptions there have evolved in a very different way from Europe.

- Kang explains that most countries in the region see China's rise as an opportunity for greater political and economic stability, rather than as a threat, as many policymakers in the United States represent it.

- *China Rising* is original in linking international relations theory with an analysis of East Asian history and identity to provide a novel critique of the theory of realism* in international relations (according to which conflict is inevitable, because states pursue their own interests in an environment defined by anarchy* at the international level) and an alternative understanding of contemporary developments.

Author's Aims

With his 2007 book, *China Rising*, David C. Kang sought to highlight the difference between East Asian and Western perspectives on Asian history and how this influences different interpretations of developments in international politics. For Kang, a major flaw in the realist approach to international relations is that it transfers assumptions based on European history to Asia, where relations have evolved in a different way. European history has been marked by several factors that are hardly present in East Asia; specifically, development in Europe and

❝ In Chinese eyes—and explicitly accepted in surrounding nations—the world of the past millennium has consisted of civilization (China) and barbarians (all other states). In this view, as long as the barbarian states were willing to kowtow to the Chinese emperor and show formal acceptance of their lower position in the hierarchy, the Chinese had neither the need to invade these countries nor the desire to do so. Explicit acceptance of the Chinese perspective on the regional order brought diplomatic recognition from China and allowed the pursuit of international trade and diplomacy. ❞

David C. Kang, *China Rising*

the West has been characterized by the emergence of the nation state,* the recognition of Westphalian sovereignty* (according to which individual states are fundamentally equal), and the practice of forming alliances and coalitions to counter the dominance of any one state ("balance of power" theory*).

International politics in East Asia has been formed completely differently, both materially and culturally. East Asian international relations were defined materially by the presence of a main power, the Chinese empire, and culturally by the acceptance of the tributary system* (a system operating from the eleventh to the nineteenth centuries in which kings from other Asian nations paid tributes to the Chinese emperor in exchange for peace and security) which legitimized and supported Chinese supremacy.

Through his analysis, Kang exposes the Eurocentric nature of contemporary international relations theory, showing that many propositions by scholars in the discipline are derived from just the last two centuries of European history. The entire body of realist and neorealist* theorization (which maintains the basic tenets of the realist tradition, such as the adversarial nature of politics, but focuses on the role of international structures and material factors) is drawn from the study of the two world wars and European history of the nineteenth century rather than from Asia's unique context.

Approach

According to Kang, China's emergence as a major economic and political power can provide an opportunity for thinkers to overcome explanations founded on the lessons of European history in order to promote a better understanding of global politics. This shift is essential to properly analyze the evolution of the regional environment in areas of the world not characterized by the same material and cultural evolution experienced in Europe.

This process of "de-Westernization" is not aimed only at freeing the discipline from its alleged cultural bias. Making sense of Asia's uniqueness and giving the right attention to material and cultural factors that shaped Asian history and politics have fundamental practical consequences.

Kang translates these aims into a clearly developed plan. He first addresses theoretical issues, such as the relationship between political ideas and material factors. He then goes on to highlight the main differences between East Asian and European history.

Here, he stresses that modern European history has been based on the so-called Westphalian system of equal, sovereign* (that is, autonomous and self-governing) states, whereas Asian nations have historically embraced Sinocentrism,* seeing China as a superior nation, expected to lead the region's growth and ensure its security. Next, he applies his theoretical approach and tests it against both long-term (1300–1900) history and recent developments in East Asian international relations, demonstrating the stabilizing effect of the Chinese rise. Ultimately, he shows how East Asian self-perceptions are very different from the dominant view of Asia in the West. He explains that most countries in the region see the strength of China as an advance toward greater political and economic stability, while the United States and its allies tend to regard it as a threat.

Contribution in Context

China Rising builds on Kang's previous research. Since the early 2000s, he has contributed to the debate on China, putting forward a number of significant theoretical arguments. For Kang, contemporary international relations theory is incapable of understanding the full reality of East Asian politics, since all of its main concepts are deduced from European history and do not necessarily apply to all contexts. He has long argued that the basic pitfall of the field, and particularly of realist approaches, was considering anarchy as a permanent and universal characteristic of international politics because of the absence of a global governing authority. He has asserted that contemporary international relations are better described by "hierarchy"*—not just in Asia but globally. In taking a position that does not view all states as equal players on the field of international politics, he positioned himself against the mainstream approach in international relations theory, especially in American academia—realism. He directly challenges the main assumptions of neorealism, namely positivism* (according to which a social fact can be known through external observation), rationalism* (according to which decisions to act are made on rational grounds, following ordered preferences), anarchy, and the tendency toward the balance of power.

Before *China Rising*, Kang directly questioned the balance of power theory. Together with the neorealist scholar William Wohlforth,* he disproved the idea that a general tendency toward a balance of power has existed in world history; the two scholars pointed out that this practice has been extremely rare in East Asia due to the existence of the Sinocentric system. Similarly, the positivist element within realism, which involves developing universally applicable "laws" through observation, was inadequate for Kang, as he found that Asian international relations did not follow the models developed through observing historical progression in Europe. Turning his back on the dominant realism has led him to embrace the main theoretical stances of the constructivist* approach, which places a central emphasis on national and regional identity in international relations.

The added value of Kang's work, and particularly of *China Rising*, is his capacity to highlight how these theoretical considerations play out through examining the long-term history of East Asian international relations. In doing so, he produces a solid alternative interpretation of the Chinese rise and its consequences.

SECTION 2
IDEAS

MODULE 5
MAIN IDEAS

KEY POINTS

- *China Rising* charts the emergence of China as a major regional and global power, and assesses the consequences of this rise for international relations.

- Kang's main argument is that due to shared Asian history and identity, East Asian countries will accommodate China's rise because they believe it will foster regional growth and stability.

- Kang presents his argument in three parts, and concludes by encouraging the United States, and other major powers, to cooperate with China rather than confront it, believing that this will promote global peace and security.

Key Themes

The central theme of David C. Kang's *China Rising* is, as the title suggests, the ascent of China as a regional and global power. Kang highlights how the emergence of China as a great power has been accommodated by other key states in the East Asian region. Moreover, the Chinese ascent has contributed to the stabilization of the region by promoting economic growth and commercial integration.

According to Kang, this contradicts conventional international relations theories, in particular realism,* which considers the rise of a great power as a cause of instability and conflict. Realism predicts that neighboring countries would feel threatened and take action to balance Chinese economic and military power. So far, according to Kang, the Chinese ascent has not led other East Asian nations to assume this confrontational stance. They consider the Chinese rise as an opportunity, rather than as a threat to their security and interests,

❝ There is no theoretical reason to think that because Europe has a history of balancing, East Asia must see balancing in the future as well. **❞**

David C. Kang, *China Rising*

looking favorably at the emergence of a strong and wealthy China as a political and economic leading state in the region. This accommodating stance is explained by two main factors: economic interdependence* and a shared Asian identity (key components of, respectively, liberal* and constructivist* theories of international relations). Kang calls on the United States and other Westerns nations to adopt a similarly cooperative relationship with China in the interest of cultivating peace and stability.

Exploring the Ideas

In *China Rising*, Kang uses a theoretical framework inspired by analytic eclecticism.* This approach explains the behavior of states as a result of a complex interplay between their power, interests, and identities. In doing so, Kang draws upon three main approaches to the study of international politics: realism, liberalism, and constructivism.

He argues that purely realist accounts of East Asian international relations, with their assumptions regarding conflict and the anarchy* of the international scene, are not sufficient to explain why China's neighbors accommodate its political and economic ascent. By focusing only on material factors, such as military power, the realist theorization ignores the role played by identity. In contrast, constructivism argues that it is impossible to understand the behavior of states without exploring the relation between the construction of a state's identity and its political choices. Being part of a Sinocentric system,* China's centrality and political superiority constitutes a significant element of the identity of Asian states. This situation results in their welcoming, rather than opposing, the renewed leadership of China in the region and its success compared with other major states.

Kang supports his position by setting out the crucial role that identity has played in the long history of East Asian international relations. He highlights how the contemporary behavior of China's neighbors is consistent with a theoretical model that predicts how a sense of shared identity will promote a recognition of shared interests. By contrast, realist models fail to explain current trends in East Asian political affairs. According to Kang, realist accounts predicting instability and conflict do not simply generate a faulty appraisal of the current state of affairs: they also contribute to biased policy options, influencing other countries, especially the United States, to consider the Chinese rise as inherently threatening and to propose policy options aimed at undermining or containing it.

It is essential to Kang that his readers understand the relationship between international relations theory and the formation of foreign policy. Emphasizing the evidence that suggests a strong China contributes to stability and growth in Asia, Kang's argument implies that the United States and other Western countries should see China's ascent as an opportunity, not as a threat. Consequently, they should enact policies aimed at accommodating China's development.

Language and Expression

Kang delivers his three-part argument in a clear, concise, and methodical manner. He engages heavily with international relations theory, but he explains realism, liberalism, and constructivism in depth, and clarifies both the strengths and weaknesses of these schools of thought. He also details key concepts of these perspectives, such as balancing power* (roughly, the formation of alliances to balance the dominance of any single nation) and bandwagoning* (a nation serving its own interests by aligning itself with a more dominant nation), making the text both relevant in its field and accessible to nonspecialist readers.

In his deep engagement with East Asian history and the development of Asian identity from 1300 to 1900, Kang introduces the idea of Sinocentrism. He breaks down this complex idea in accessible terms, showing how this tradition helps East Asian countries see China's rise as both natural and legitimate, and as an opportunity rather than a threat.

Many scholars and politicians downplay the role of ideas and identity in international relations. The simplistic presumption that China's rise will destabilize the region and the world has led a number of Western nations to act in ways that safeguard US power and influence. For Kang, this Westerncentric stance demands great scrutiny. The author therefore challenges this position and offers a new understanding of China, suggesting that the US should reevaluate its foreign policy in Asia and cooperate with China.

MODULE 6
SECONDARY IDEAS

KEY POINTS

- *China Rising* fundamentally critiques Eurocentric* theories of international relations that are likely to overlook the idiosyncrasies of Asian identity that mean East Asian states do not feel threatened by China's rise.

- Kang points out that US foreign policy based on traditional international relations theories will not be effective. He gives voice to the opinion in many Asian countries that China is a more reliable and beneficial ally than the United States.

- Kang tries to build an argument for a future US foreign policy of cooperation with China and the rest of East Asia where all participants benefit and no one "wins" at the expense of another.

Other Ideas

At the heart of David C. Kang's approach to international relations in *China Rising* is his critique of the Eurocentric nature of the field itself. He explains that European- and American-biased theories of international relations are poorly equipped to deal with Asia and its long-term history and identity. While Europeans' historical emphasis has been on preventing the reign of one major power, and nations have tended to form alliances so that power might be balanced, this model does not transfer to the Asian context in a straightforward way. Within international relations theory, a growing number of scholars and commentators have begun to recognize the importance of regional traditions, ideas, and idiosyncrasies. Kang and his like-minded colleagues have attempted to move toward an analytical framework that accounts for the peculiarities of international relations in Asia.

❝ For too long international relations scholars have derived theoretical propositions from European experience and then treated them as deductive and universal. ❞

David C. Kang, *China Rising*

A strong link between Kang's method and his message is visible here. He provides a model of a different way of thinking about international politics and the potential consequences of a rising power by emphasizing a non-Western perspective. At the same time, he asserts that an appreciation of Asia's unique history and context is essential for other global powers to adjust to a global landscape that includes a strong Chinese state, and to derive the potential benefits of China's success through cooperation rather than suspicion, containment,* and conflict.

Simplistically transposing European international relations theory onto the Asian context, for Kang, seems more likely to inflame tensions than to promote peace and prosperity in the region. Balance of power theory,* developed using an analysis of European history, has motivated a strategy that involves maintaining an active US military presence in Asia and actively forming alliances with other Asian nations to balance China's influence. Policies formed without taking Asia's history and identity into consideration are, for Kang, misguided. Furthermore, he argues that many Asian countries see Washington as a less-than-trustworthy ally, and feel more secure reinforcing their relations with Beijing.

Exploring the Ideas

The main concepts and theories of international relations, especially realist* theories, stem from the study of European politics in the nineteenth and twentieth centuries, or from relations between great powers in the second half of the twentieth century. European states have preserved a balance of power, trying to prevent states, such as Napoleonic France* (the dominant power in much of continental Europe in the early nineteenth century, ruled by the military leader Napoleon Bonaparte*) and Nazi Germany* (Germany under the extremely right-wing rule of Adolf Hitler's* Nazi Party from 1933 to 1945), from achieving regional hegemony*—that is, political dominance. Focusing mainly on material factors (such as military capabilities, economic and natural resources, and so on), realist theories assume that a balance of power is a natural and necessary outcome over the long term.[1]

Both the Westphalian system of sovereignty*—which considers nations both independent of and fundamentally equal to each other, at least in theory—and the Sinocentric system*—within which there is a recognized regional hierarchy,* with China at the top—are based on a particular interplay between power, interests, and identities, and each formed over history in a particular context. Scholars, therefore, should be careful never to overlook the role of identity and ideas in shaping relations between states.

Since the early 2000s, Kang has made a particularly important contribution to the debate on the uniqueness of East Asian international politics and on the alleged ethnocentrism* of international relations theories.[2] *China Rising* is a contribution to, and a continuation of, earlier critiques of the ethnocentric* nature of international relations theory (that is, theory founded on the historical experience of a particular people). Kang joins scholars such as the political scientists Barry Buzan* and Amitav Acharya* wishing to move toward an approach that challenges ethnocentrism. Indeed, Kang, Buzan, and Acharya have discussed the possibility of elaborating an "Asian theory of international relations" to this end.[3]

Another relevant argument concerns the particular role of the United States in international relations. As Kang's analysis shows, East

Asian states do not feel threatened by China's rise due to their historically shared identity and interests. However, both liberal* and realist studies claim that the military and political presence of US forces, as well as the network of alliances that link Washington with the main actors in the region, are the fundamental precondition for Asian peace and stability.[4]

Kang points out the consequences of American foreign policy, highlighting how two American administrations failed to reassure their Asian partners, ultimately allowing China to reemerge as the primary source of leadership and guidance for countries in the region. According to Kang, the American response to the Asian financial crisis* of 1997, allowing states to suffer huge economic losses, even bankruptcy,[5] and the country's questionable actions within the so-called war on terror* (US military actions in the developing world following the terror attacks of September 11, 2001, known as "9/11"*) have damaged their ability to present the United States as a stabilizing force. Many Asian states are suspicious of the United States either as a global hegemon (dominant power) willing to impose its own interests and agenda outside its borders, or as unable to provide aid when it is needed most. This both undermined Asian states' trust in Washington and helped consolidate the idea of China as the future political and economic leader at the regional level.

Overlooked

The most overlooked part of *China Rising* is Kang's hypotheses on the future role of the United States in East Asia. He seeks to describe a scenario in which Chinese ascendancy creates a positive-sum game,* involving China, other Asian states, and the United States—that is, a situation in which no player "wins" at the expense of any other. He sees Beijing's ascendancy and the expansion of China's economic and political role as a potential source of stability and economic growth, regionally and globally.

In the final part of the book, Kang throws the spotlight onto the rapid deterioration of Washington's political and military dominance. All the trends Kang explores in the book can be interpreted as signs of a declining influence of the United States in Asia. China is reemerging as regional leader, and other states recognize the legitimacy of its leadership for cultural, historical, and economic reasons.

Recently, the United States attempted to reassert its primacy in Asia. President Obama's* administration is attempting to reinforce economic, diplomatic, and military relations with Japan, Korea, and Australia, and to create new partnerships with former adversaries such as Myanmar and Vietnam.

In Kang's view, most Asian states in the longer term will face a choice between aligning themselves with the rising China or the declining United States. Since China will likely continue to be a powerful engine of future economic growth and, above all, because of the heritage of the Sinocentric system, loyalty to Beijing over Washington will probably prevail as the more attractive choice.

NOTES

1   Kenneth N. Waltz, "The Emerging Structure of International Politics," *International Security* 18, no. 2 (1993): 44–79; for a critique see Paul Schroeder, "Historical Reality vs. Neo-Realist Theory," *International Security* 19, no. 1 (1994): 108–48.

2   David C. Kang, "Getting Asia Wrong: The Need for New Analytical Frameworks," *International Security* 27, no. 4 (2003): 57–85; David C. Kang, "Hierarchy, Balancing, and Empirical Puzzles in Asian International Relations," *International Security* 28, no. 3 (2004): 165–80; David C. Kang, "Hierarchy in Asian International Relations: 1300–1900," *Asian Security* 1, no. 1 (2005): 53–79.

3   Amitav Acharya and Barry Buzan, "Why Is There No Non-Western International Relations Theory? An Introduction," *International Relations of the Asia-Pacific* 7, no. 3 (2007): 287–312; Amitav Acharya, "Will Asia's Past Be Its Future?" *International Security* 28, no. 3 (2004): 149–64.

4   G. John Ikenberry, "Power and Liberal Order: America's Postwar World Order in Transition," *International Relations of the Asia-Pacific* 5, no. 2 (2005): 133–52; Thomas J. Christensen, "Fostering Stability or Creating a Monster? The Rise of China and US Policy toward East Asia," *International Security* 31, no. 1 (2006): 81–126; Victor D. Cha, "Complex Patchworks: US Alliances as Part of Asia's Regional Architecture," *Asia Policy* 11 (2011): 27–50.

5   The United States responded to the Asian Financial Crisis through the International Monetary Fund and the World Bank. However, according to Kang, American support was perceived as hesitant and insufficient.

MODULE 7
ACHIEVEMENT

KEY POINTS

- *China Rising* has made an important contribution to international relations theory and the study of Asian politics, and has attracted the attention of leading international historians.

- *China Rising* is extremely timely, analyzing an ongoing and momentous shift in the contemporary geopolitical landscape and in academic practice.

- Kang's vision faces significant challenges from many policy-makers in the United States who see China as a competitor and a threat, and therefore wish to contain its rise.

Assessing the Argument

David C. Kang's *China Rising* has made an important contribution to international relations theory and the study of East Asian politics. More, the work has been influential in shaping wider political debates on foreign policy and international affairs, especially with regard to the future relationship between the West and China.

Kang's work has not only influenced international relations theorists, having had a notable impact on international historians. The author's thesis on the possible return of a Sinocentric* system in Asia, in which Asian countries see China's rise as historically legitimate and an engine of economic growth and stability for the region, has attracted significant attention. One international relations scholar has referenced Kang's work in describing the tributary system* of the eleventh to the nineteenth centuries, under which kings from other Asian nations paid tributes to the Chinese emperor in exchange for

❝ Directly explaining why East Asian nations have accommodated China's rise, and why balance of power politics has not emerged, is important theoretically because it is interests and identity, not power, that are the key variables in determining threat and stability in international relations. ❞

David C. Kang, *China Rising*

peace and security, as the "basic premise of modern Asia."[1] Other historians have questioned whether the Sinocentric system was actually peaceful, highlighting important historical conflicts. Another scholar, for example, recently defined the "tribute system" as a "comforting fiction" that obscures unequal and coercive historical and contemporary relations between China and other Asian nations.[2]

Kang's influence on historians of China and of international history more broadly is meaningful, even if it is rather limited in scope. International relations theory and international history often perceive themselves as completely separate and non-communicating disciplines. But the fact that both historians and international relations theorists are discussing such themes as Sinocentrism and the uniqueness of East Asian history is a sign of progress for both disciplines, and confirmation of the importance of Kang's work.

Achievement in Context

China's rise to global prominence constitutes a significant shift in world affairs, bringing it to the forefront of international news, as well as debates among policymakers and academics. Kang's work provides a timely and coherent alternative to the mainstream view at present that portrays China's rise as a threat to American dominance and the East Asian region. The author has consistently argued against the expansion of the United States' military presence in the region and the use of force to resolve diplomatic controversies such as the North Korean nuclear issue.

Much of Kang's audience encounters his work through his contributions in major newspapers such as the *New York Times*. In a series of opinion pieces, he has taken on the views of Korean American scholar Victor Cha. Since 2002, the two have engaged in a fruitful, ongoing debate about the relationship between the United States and China, and the United States and North Korea. In these pieces, Kang has repeatedly argued that the US should cooperate with China rather than confront it, while Cha takes a more combative stance on the issue.

Kang's call for the West to regard China as a valuable partner rather than an enemy may have received a more meaningful engagement within the general public and fellow scholars than among US policymakers. So far, the Obama* administration seems to be continuing the policy position of his predecessors, maintaining the US economic and military presence in Asia in an effort to contain the growth of Chinese power and influence. The administration has, for example, increased military budgets in the region and sought to strengthen commercial and military ties with Japan, South Korea, and Australia.[3]

Limitations

Since Kang's central assertion is that cooperation with China is both potentially beneficial and entirely feasible, the existing tensions between the United States and China threaten to undermine his thesis entirely. In an entirely different analysis of China's development, the international relations scholar John Mearsheimer* believes that the most effective way for China to expand its power and security is to achieve regional dominance in Asia. To accomplish this, it will not only need to be the most powerful economic player in the region, but it will also need to establish military supremacy. He predicts that China will take action to resolve ongoing disputes over territory and natural resources while at the same time reducing US influence in Asia by pushing the US navy out of strategic waters.

Mearsheimer's position is that the United States should activate a policy of containment* to arrest China's pursuit of regional hegemony.* He does not think it should use preemptive war to achieve this because the potential consequences would be too great. However, he does believe the United States should promote a balance of power* by reinforcing commercial ties and both reinforcing existing military alliances and developing new ones.

In the long run, however, Mearsheimer does not believe that containment will work, due to the intense competition between the two countries. Under these conditions, Mearsheimer sees war as practically inevitable. This may be provoked by the need for the United States to intervene to protect the interests of another regional player, such as Taiwan. In strong contrast to Kang's position, which views cooperative coexistence as a viable possibility, Mearsheimer insists that neither Sinocentrism nor economic interdependence* will prevent intense security competition and war.[4]

This argument, if proven right, in part or as a whole, will expose limitations in Kang's thesis.

NOTES

1   Takeshi Hamashita, *China, East Asia and the Global Economy: Regional and Historical Perspectives* (Abingdon: Routledge, 2013), 14.

2   Kirk Larsen, "Comforting Fictions: The Tribute System, the Westphalian Order, and Sino-Korean Relations," *Journal of East Asian Studies* 13, no. 2 (2013): 233–57.

3   Michael D. Swaine, "Chinese Leadership and Elite Responses to the US Pacific Pivot," *China Leadership Monitor* 38 (2012): 1–26.

4   John Mearsheimer, *The Tragedy of Great Power Politics* (New York: W. W. & Norton Company, 2001).

MODULE 8
PLACE IN THE AUTHOR'S WORK

KEY POINTS

- In David C. Kang's body of work, he consistently highlights the Eurocentric* nature of academic research on Asian history and international relations.

- *China Rising* reinforces this argument by detailing the shared history and identity of East Asian cultures, and arguing that, unlike many Western nations, countries in the region see China's ascent as beneficial, natural, and legitimate.

- Kang's body of work poses a convincing challenge to realist* scholarship in international relations, and presents an alternative understanding of China, useful to both academics and policymakers.

Positioning

China Rising is the third and probably most influential book written by David C. Kang. It builds on the long-standing areas of interest explored in his earlier books, journalism, and scholarly articles, including the peculiarities of East Asia, the concept of hierarchy,* and the role of ideas and culture in East Asian international relations.[1] The book is regarded as an important contribution to debate on the nature of contemporary Asian politics. Kang is considered one of the key proponents of a policy of engagement toward Beijing and an outspoken critic of a policy of containment* of China's rise.

In his 2003 article "Getting Asia Wrong," Kang laid out the foundation for *China Rising* by making two key arguments. First, European theories in general, and realist theories in particular, are often ill-suited to analyzing the nature of Asian international relations.

❝ Using a broad historical context, current regional issues and domestic political concerns, Kang presents an empirically exhaustive study of the region, arriving at the conclusion that East Asia is responding favorably to China's rise. ❞

Stefan Fergus,* "Book Review: David C. Kang, *China Rising: Peace, Power and Order in East Asia*"

Second, scholars must create non-Eurocentric analytical frameworks and be more rigorous in their analyses of Asian history and international relations.

China Rising moves beyond his prior work by providing a theoretically and empirically sound analysis of the consequences of the rise of China as a regional and global power. Kang concludes that, contrary to the prevailing view in academia and politics, countries in the region see China's success as legitimate because of the tradition of Sinocentrism,* and this positive arrangement, if it continues, represents hope for greater stability in the region and the wider world.

Integration

In the work that followed *China Rising*, Kang confirmed his position and reiterated his main theoretical arguments, such as the centrality of identity in international relations, the role of hierarchy in East Asia, and the stabilizing effect of China's rise. In *East Asia before the West: Five Centuries of Trade and Tribute*, published in 2010, a work Kang himself presents as a continuation of *China Rising*, he further explores the formation of the tributary system* that dominated East Asia between 1300 and 1900, stressing how this system influenced the development of the East Asian order before the interruption of Western colonizers in the late nineteenth century.

Kang shows how, during this period, China had just two large-scale conflicts with its neighbors, Korea, Vietnam, and Japan. Otherwise, it was a largely peaceful time, characterized by strong diplomatic and commercial ties. He contrasts this with the Westphalian system* in Europe, which was characterized by formal equality between states and a balance of power* strategy. Unlike the Asian Sinocentric system, European under the Westphalian system experienced incessant interstate conflicts.

Throughout his work, Kang portrays the Asian system as one that should be considered unique, and appreciated and analyzed as such. He concludes that shared history and identity are absolutely fundamental, and the acceptance of China as a natural and legitimate leader on the part of its Asian neighbors is, for Kang, clear evidence of this.

Significance

The publication of *China Rising* brought about an important turning point in Kang's career. It has contributed to spreading Kang's ideas and concepts to a broader public and has made him a major protagonist in the debate on the nature of China's rise, and the consequences of this, in the United States. The book's success has helped establish Kang as one of the most influential American intellectual supporters of a welcoming stance toward China and one of the most outspoken critics of the "China threat theory."[2]

David C. Kang is one of the most visible and convincing supporters of a policy of engagement with Beijing and the adoption of a strategy aimed at building positive and close relations between the United States and China. Although his influence is clearly present in the scholarly debate, Kang's position does not represent the mainstream in the academic or political debates. Increasingly, both the American administration and the scholarly community are highlighting the potential drawbacks of the presence of an economically and politically strong China.[3]

Overall, however, Kang's voice is widely acknowledged as one of the most original, lucid, and credible within this debate, and he is likely to continue to be so for the foreseeable future. At present, Kang's work continues through several research projects focused on topics relating to East Asian politics, such as the evolution of the North Korean security situation and military developments in Asia.

NOTES

1   David C. Kang, "Hierarchy, Balancing, and Empirical Puzzles in Asian International Relations," *International Security* 28, no. 3 (2003): 165–80; David C. Kang, "The Theoretical Roots of Hierarchy in International Relations," *Australian Journal of International Affairs* 58, no. 3 (2004): 337–52; David C. Kang, "Hierarchy in Asian International Relations: 1300–1900," *Asian Security* 1, no. 1 (2005): 53–79.

2   Yi Edward Yang and Xinsheng Liu, "The 'China Threat' through the Lens of US Print Media: 1992–2006," *Journal of Contemporary China* 21, no. 76 (2012): 695–711; Chikako Ueki, "The Rise of 'China Threat' Arguments" (PhD diss., Massachusetts Institute of Technology, 2006); Emma V. Broomfield, "Perceptions of Danger: The China Threat Theory," *Journal of Contemporary China* 12, no. 35 (2003): 265–84.

3   Evelyn Goh, "The United States in Asia: Reflections on Deterrence, Alliances, and the 'Balance' of Power," *International Relations of the Asia-Pacific* 12, no. 3 (2012): 511–18.

SECTION 3
IMPACT

MODULE 9
THE FIRST RESPONSES

KEY POINTS

- Beyond the opposition from the realist* school of international relations, Kang's position is vulnerable to arguments pointing out that China's current military conflicts in Asia, volatile global financial markets, and popular uprisings may undermine China's rise.

- Since *China Rising*, Kang has continued to produce work founded on his core thesis concerning the importance of Sinocentrism* in relation to China's rise and future.

- The centrality of the Chinese economy in current affairs provided a broad and receptive audience for *China Rising*.

Criticism

Perhaps predictably, David C. Kang's *China Rising* has met notable criticisms from realist scholars of international relations. Some have argued that Asian states' willingness to accommodate China's rise has more to do with their potential access to American military protection (in cases of conflict over disputed territory, for example) than to Sinocentrism. Realists' criticisms have built on a vast body of theoretical literature on alliances, deterrence* (the understanding that the threat of overwhelming military action preserves the peace), and diplomacy, and on several empirical analyses of East Asian politics.[1] Other scholars, the most prominent of which is John Mearsheimer,* have suggested that Kang underestimates the intensity of the competition between the United States and China, and the resulting tension makes a US strategy of containment* and future conflict inevitable.[2]

" **What is wrong with this picture? Nothing—at least with regard to the fifteen years that Kang studied. Although Kang has done an excellent and important job, one weakness of relying too much on a constructivist approach is that norms and identities are often more vulnerable to sudden change than analysts might assume.** "

Peter Van Nees, "Anticipating the Unexpected"

On a more fundamental level, Kang's treatment of facts in *China Rising* has been called into question. Some critics argue that China's rise has already caused several military reactions. For example, the United States and Japan have been renewing and deepening their alliance, and Japan has progressively abandoned its postwar pacifism.[3] Moreover, the general level of military expenses in the region has been rising dramatically. China is also involved in a number of territorial disputes with almost all of its neighboring countries, from Tibet to the South and East China Seas.[4]

Another significant blind spot that critics have identified in Kang's argument is the possibility that China's rise will be undermined by economic difficulties, or other hard-to-predict elements, in the future. According to the international relations scholar Peter Van Ness,* for example, China could face a decline of legitimacy related to an economic slowdown or internal unrest over issues such as human rights. Consequently, Van Ness believes that Kang relies too heavily on constructivist* theory, emphasizing the socially constructed nature of a state's identity, and does not consider that volatile conditions could make China's future behavior unpredictable.[5]

Responses

Since *China Rising*, Kang has published one book and several journal articles on China's ascent and the uniqueness of Asian international politics.[6] Throughout his work, his approach and central thesis remain consistent.

In *Asia before the West: Five Centuries of Trade and Tribute* (2010), he explores in greater detail the nature of the tributary system* that defined East Asian politics before the imposition of Western colonialism. He argues that the Sinocentric order was regulated by a complex set of rules and institutions that stabilized the region. China's hegemony,* contrary to the formal equality that existed among European nation states* under the Westphalian system,* guaranteed peace and economic development. In his later article "International Relations Theory and East Asian History," he emphasizes how the perceived legitimacy of Chinese centrality was an essential element of pre-colonial politics in East Asia.

Kang's work since *China Rising* has not explicitly addressed any criticisms of the book. Instead, he has persistently argued in favor of the thesis he proposed in *China Rising* in its entirety. Kang's scholarship and the debate on his work reflect the present polarization in the field of international relations between realists, liberals,* and constructivists.

Kang has dismissed realist criticisms in two ways. First, he has continued to break down the ways in which the concept and the practice of balance of power,* though prominent in Europe, does not fit the Asian political and cultural heritage. Kang establishes his conclusion that Asian nations are accommodating toward China's ascent by retaining a position that uses trends in Asian history—rather than European history—to analyze the contemporary Asian context. Second, he claims the credit for the peaceful nature of China's rise lies with the country's perceived legitimacy in the region rather than with America's military presence.

Conflict and Consensus

The enduring relevance of Kang's work is grounded in its solid theoretical counterargument to the mainstream view in international relations theory and policy debates. In the United States particularly, the debate on the rise of China is framed mainly through the intellectual lens provided by the realist approach to international relations.

Realists tend to view the rise of a new power as a dangerous, destabilizing force, and China's current prominence suggests that it could achieve a position at the top of political hierarchies* in Asia, if not globally. This school of thought emphasizes the anarchic* nature of international politics, and so with no global governmental authority regulating international relations, the pressure generated by the military capabilities of both sides will probably lead Washington to consider Beijing as a threat to both its dominance and the security of Asia. Inevitably, according to realist mainstream predictions, China will translate its increased economic power into an escalation of its military capabilities, and will try to coerce its neighbors into making alliances with it rather than the United States. Consequently, balancing or containing the rise of China is considered the most sensible strategy in response to the challenge represented by China's rise.[7]

However, Kang's work, which draws from the liberal and constructivist traditions, presents an entirely different picture. He argues that a stronger China will foster stability and increase prosperity both within China and in the region as a whole—a situation that has been, and will continue to be, welcomed by China's neighbors. From Kang's perspective, the best policy stance for the West to secure global security amid China's rise is one of cooperation, not containment or confrontation.

NOTES

1   Thomas J. Christensen, *Worse than a Monolith: Alliance Politics and Problems of Coercive Diplomacy in Asia* (Princeton, NJ: Princeton University Press, 2011); Alexander L. George and Richard Smoke, "Deterrence and Foreign Policy," *World Politics* 41, no. 2 (1989): 170–82; Glenn H. Snyder, *Alliance Politics* (Ithaca, NY: Cornell University Press, 2007).

2   Aaron L. Friedberg, "Ripe for Rivalry: Prospects for Peace in a Multipolar Asia," *International Security* 18, no. 3 (1993): 5–33; John J. Mearsheimer, "China's Unpeaceful Rise," *Current History* 105, no. 690 (2006): 160–2.

3   Richard J. Samuels, *Securing Japan: Tokyo's Grand Strategy and the Future of East Asia* (Ithaca, NY: Cornell University Press, 2007); Christopher W. Hughes, *Japan's Remilitarisation* (Abingdon: Routledge for International Institute for Strategic Studies, 2009).

4   M. Taylor Fravel, "Regime Insecurity and International Cooperation: Explaining China's Compromises in Territorial Disputes," *International Security* 30, no. 2 (2005): 46–83.

5   Peter Van Ness, "Anticipating the Unexpected," *Asia Policy* 6 (2008): 168–72.

6   David C. Kang, *East Asia before the West: Five Centuries of Trade and Tribute* (New York: Columbia University Press, 2010); David C. Kang, "Hierarchy and Legitimacy in International Systems: The Tribute System in Early Modern East Asia," *Security Studies* 19, no. 4 (2010): 591–622; David C. Kang, "International Relations Theory and East Asian History: An Overview," *Journal of East Asian Studies* 13, no. 2 (2013): 181–205; David C. Kang, "Authority and Legitimacy in International Relations: Evidence from Korean and Japanese Relations in Pre-modern East Asia," *The Chinese Journal of International Politics* 5, no. 1 (2012): 55–71.

7   John J. Mearsheimer, *The Tragedy of Great Power Politics* (New York: W. W. Norton & Company, 2001); John J. Mearsheimer, "China's Unpeaceful Rise," *Current History* 105, no. 690 (2006): 160–2.

MODULE 10
THE EVOLVING DEBATE

KEY POINTS

- *China Rising* draws attention to the Eurocentric*
  nature of international relations scholarship, and uses
  unconventional analytical frameworks to understand the
  complexities of Asian politics.

- Kang analyzes the history of Sinocentrism* and presents
  this tradition as the principal factor establishing China as a
  natural leader in Asia.

- Kang's assessment of East Asian politics and the
  relationship between China and the United States presents
  a formidable challenge to the realist* mainstream, which
  views China's rise as inherently destabilizing.

Uses and Problems

The Eurocentric nature of international relations is a key issue that
David C. Kang's *China Rising* has brought to the foreground of debate
in his field. As Kang has made clear, the analysis of international politics
outside the Western world might require different analytical
frameworks beyond those formed in Europe and the United States
through the analysis of Western history.

China Rising, along with Kang's subsequent book *Asia before the
West: Five Centuries of Trade and Tribute*, approaches its subject matter
with an emphasis on the uniqueness of Asian history, identity, and
political dynamics, and makes its predictions for the region on this
basis. The possibility, presented by Kang, that China could recreate
something comparable to the Sinocentric order of years past has
stoked lively debate in the field of international politics.

Kang's appraisal of international relations in Asia creates a robust
alternative to realist assessments, which focus on the potential dangers

❝ *China Rising* is an important book because Kang takes up the challenge of addressing a much-discussed topic from an explicitly regional perspective and through a theory of East Asian international relations. The book is additionally useful because it revives interest in the fundamental problem of how to theorize power, interest, and identity. *China Rising* should thus spur other scholars of East Asian IR toward work that can overcome the dichotomy between foreign policy and international relations theory and place East Asian IR at the forefront of challenging and extending IR theories. ❞

Evelyn Goh,* "Power, Interest, and Identity: Reviving the Sinocentric Hierarchy in East Asia"

of China's rise. The author has consistently challenged realism both theoretically and empirically (that is, through an analysis of observable evidence). On the one hand, he has adopted an essentially constructivist* point of view, stressing how Asian states' acceptance of China's rise cannot be explained without understanding the peculiarities of their identities and the historical legacy of the Sinocentric system. Realism, in contrast, stresses the intensity of the existing competition between the United States and China, and predicts armed conflict over economic and military supremacy as practically inevitable.

Schools of Thought

While his analysis is widely regarded as original and valuable, David C. Kang's work has not produced an entirely new school of thought. Rather, it has made an important contribution to the study of Asian politics within international relations theory, and offered an alternative perspective on the ascent of China as a major global power.

China Rising employs a combination of liberal* and constructivist methods. It follows liberalism insofar as Kang stresses the importance of economic exchange and interdependence* in maintaining peace and security. Liberalism was the dominant theory in international relations from World War I* to World War II,* and has been reinvigorated since the 1970s to explain how nations as trade partners operate within international politics. Kang's approach is also informed by the constructivist stance in his focus on Asian countries' unique history and identity, which, he believes, has accommodated a reemergence of a Sinocentric system that welcomes China as a leader in the region. This argument has provoked considerable attention and debate, and provides a unique analytical approach for understanding current developments in international relations.

This directly contrasts with realist scholarship, which argues that identity and economic interdependence are only marginally important. Rather, realists believe that states tend generally to take action that would advance their power and secure their position in an intensely competitive environment characterized by the absence of a higher global governing authority. In the case of Asia, realist theorists predict that economic and military competition will inevitably lead to conflict between the United States and China, and even potentially war.

In Current Scholarship

Several of the ideas advanced in *China Rising* have provided a springboard for innovative thinking on Asian politics. Theorists Steve Chan* and Reinhard Drifte* are among the scholars who have engaged with Kang in the current debate on whether Asian states are balancing China's rise or accommodating it.[1] Chan has built on the foundations set in *China Rising* by further investigating the relations between China and other East Asian states, while Drifte has done the same by examining relations between China and Japan since the end of the Cold War.* Both have confirmed Kang's thesis on the absence of a balance of power* against China.

Other scholars have engaged with Kang's idea of a possible return of a Sinocentric order in East Asia as a consequence of China's rise. For example, the scholar of Chinese politics William A. Callahan* has analyzed key concepts that China uses to justify its growing centrality in Asia and its alleged position of superiority in relation to other Asian states.[2] Linsay Cunningham-Cross* has further explored the relationship between contemporary Chinese political strategy and historical institutional arrangements and practices. Cunningham-Cross has developed the idea, already present in the work of both Kang and the historian John K. Fairbank,* that current Chinese leaders are using their imperial past as a source of legitimacy for their future role of hegemon*— dominant power—in the region.[3]

Echoing Kang's call for a shift away from Eurocentrism in international relations theory, Zhang Feng* has discussed the possibility of generating a "Chinese theory of international relations" based on Chinese ancient philosophy, incorporating the concepts of Sinocentrism and the tributary system,* among other elements. Like Kang, he believes that a shift away from theories of international relations derived from the study of European history is necessary to fully grasp the complexities of the Asian context.

NOTES

1 Steve Chan, "An Odd Thing Happened on the Way to Balancing: East Asian States' Reactions to China's Rise," *International Studies Review* 12, no. 3 (2010), 387–412; Reinhard Drifte, *Japan's Security Relations with China since 1989: From Balancing to Bandwagoning?* (Abingdon: Routledge, 2012).

2 William A. Callahan, "Chinese Visions of World Order: Post-Hegemonic or a New Hegemony?" *International Studies Review* 10, no. 4 (2008): 749–61.

3 Linsay Cunningham-Cross, "Using the Past to (Re)Write the Future: Yan Xuetong, Pre-Qin Thought and China's Rise to Power," *China Information* 26, no. 2 (2012): 219–33.

MODULE 11
IMPACT AND INFLUENCE TODAY

KEY POINTS

- *China Rising* has proven influential in debates within academia and politics regarding the relationship between the United States and China, and China and other Asian states.

- Realist* theories of international relations, which focus on the danger posed by the rise of a new global power and the inevitability of conflict, continue to pose a distinct challenge to Kang's thesis.

- Kang has consistently argued that economic interdependence* and shared history and identity have inspired Asian neighbors to accept the legitimacy of China's leadership, and advises the West to cooperate with China rather than seek to contain its rise.

Position

China Rising has provided a substantial counterbalance to the realist mainstream position in debates within academia and politics. Its explanation of modern Asian history and the cultural particularities of Asian international relations has contributed significantly to the general understanding of Asian politics in the West. Consideration of the traditions of intra-Asian relations highlighted by Kang has brought a new level of sophistication to the analysis of the relationship between China and the United States. It has done this by providing a solid theoretical and empirical analysis, which focuses on the enduring relevance of Sinocentrism* and the Asian tributary system,* the flaws in Eurocentric* bias in international relations theory, and the unsuitability of realist theories of international relations to adequately grasp the potential benefits of China's rise.

> **❝ Although Kang's main target is international relations theory, his conclusions are highly relevant to US foreign policy. ❞**
>
> Ellen L. Frost, "Shifting the Burden of Proof"

In addition to its academic and popular readership, *China Rising* also implicitly addresses policymakers in Asia and the United States. Kang advises governments, and particularly the American government, to give up an aggressive stance toward China and recognize the mutual benefits of partnership with a strong international ally. At the time of the book's publication, with the United States led by President George W. Bush,* American foreign-policy debate was focused primarily on the Middle East; however, more recently, under President Barack Obama,* China's economic and global influence has continued to grow, and US policy has reflected this. Since 2009, the Obama administration has promoted a comprehensive reorientation of its foreign policy, reducing its commitments in the Middle East and increasing its engagement in the Asia-Pacific region, which is now considered essential for defending the United States' future power, influence, and security in the world, and for promoting global economic peace and stability.[1]

While this important shift toward Asia does not necessarily involve an overt policy of containment,* it includes several competitive strategies aimed at strengthening American economic, diplomatic, and military primacy in the region.[2]

Interaction

China Rising addresses what is arguably the most important contemporary debate in foreign affairs—the nature and potential consequences of China's rise. In doing so, it challenges the dominant view in academia and politics that China's ascent poses a threat to American primacy, and to the peace and stability of Asia.

Realist scholars interpret the rise of a new great power in international relations as a challenge to the existing order, and argue that if China's ascent is not contained, it could lead to a serious conflict, even war. Kang strongly disagrees with this take on international affairs, relying instead on liberal* and constructivist* interpretations of contemporary developments. Through a convincing analysis of the East Asian context, he highlights the stabilizing effect of China's rise and the cultural factors that induce Asian states to accommodate this development.

From the realist perspective, power politics—the tendency of sovereign* states to defend their own interests aggressively—is a major driver of state policy, and China is no exception.[3] Leading on from this position, many of Kang's critics believe that the arguments Kang presents are not necessarily at odds with realism and not completely divorced from the idea of power politics. However, they claim that some Asian states are indeed forgoing Sinocentric loyalty and aligning more closely with the United States because they fear that China represents a threat to their sovereignty.[4]

Kang's analysis of Sino-American relations is particularly critical of the Bill Clinton* and George W. Bush* administrations. The former, he argues, pressured most Southeast Asian states to open their markets but did not provide any significant help during the 1997 Asian financial crisis,* while the latter showed little sensitivity toward Muslim countries such as Indonesia in promoting its global war on terror.*

The Continuing Debate

The field of international relations theory continues to accommodate thinkers from a diverse spectrum of approaches, and a distinct divide remains between realist scholars on the one side, and both liberal and constructivists on the other. Like the geopolitical scene itself, the debate over the most accurate and productive approaches to international relations theory is constantly evolving.

Kang's work has provoked considerable reflection in the field about the need to consider new analytical frameworks to understand historical and contemporary developments in Asia, and account for the unique identities of each nation. Without this, there is a tendency to follow a Eurocentric path based on assumptions derived from patterns in European history, in particular Westphalian sovereignty*—a form of nation-state* authority that guarantees that the legitimate ruler of a country can exercise exclusive power over their territory and population, free from external interference.

Without Kang's intervention in *China Rising* the potential relevance of the Sinocentric tradition in Asian history might have been lost in the debate about China in relation to global politics. His detailed consideration of Asian history, culture, and identity, which resists the intervention of Eurocentric assumptions, presents a potent challenge to the dominant discourse in American and European academia and politics that considers China's rise necessarily destabilizing and a threat to the West.

Kang is by no means alone in promoting a liberal and constructivist view of Asian politics. In fact, international relations scholars such as Barry Buzan* and Amitav Acharya* have also questioned the extent to which realism can explain current developments. They also defend the importance of history, culture, and identity, and the uniqueness of each context.

The debate between realists, liberals, and constructivists will likely continue to evolve to include enhanced ways of interpreting world politics. Kang's work exemplifies the benefits of considering the central concepts within each approach and weighing the importance of different factors, including power, security, economic interdependence, the role of international institutions, and identity.

NOTES

1   Daniel Drezner, "Does Obama Have a Grand Strategy? Why We Need Doctrines in Uncertain Times," *Foreign Affairs* 90, no. 4 (2011): 57–62.

2   Robert S. Ross, "The Problem with the Pivot," *Foreign Affairs* 91, no. 6 (2012); Bonnie S. Glaser, "Pivot to Asia: Prepare for Unintended Consequences," in *2012 Global Forecast, Risk, Opportunity and the Next Administration*, ed. Craig Cohen and Josiane Gabel (Washington, DC: Center for Strategic and International Studies, 2012), 22–4; David Shambaugh, "Assessing the US Pivot to Asia," *Strategic Studies Quarterly* 7, no. 2 (2013): 10–19; Mark E. Manyin, *Pivot to the Pacific? The Obama Administration's "Rebalancing" toward Asia* (Washington, DC: Congressional Research Service, 2012).

3   Christopher P. Twomey, "Balancing Identity and Reality," *Asia Policy* 6 (2008): 157–61; Deborah Welch Larson and Alexei Shevchenko, "Status Seekers: Chinese and Russian Responses to US Primacy," *International Security* 34, no. 4 (2010): 63–95.

4   Twomey, "Balancing Identity and Reality."

MODULE 12
WHERE NEXT?

KEY POINTS

- *China Rising* provides an important theoretical and empirical contribution to debates on China's rise, and its relationship with the United States and its Asian neighbors.

- The text is likely to continue to influence academic and political debates on the nature and consequences of China's rise.

- One area that will likely attract more interest is the extent to which China can shape a new world order based on its particular identity and vision of international politics.

Potential

David C. Kang's *China Rising* brings an innovative, robust framework to the study of China's role in East Asia and the wider world, one whose relevance is likely to endure. To date, international relations theory, dominated by a Western perspective, has mainly considered how the United States and Europe have integrated China into the Western order. Several scholars have highlighted how China has adapted both its behavior and domestic institutions in order to integrate into the international economic and financial system.[1] Recent research, however, has also begun to predict that China's rise may entail a process of "sinicization,"* in which other nations are at China's mercy due to its economic supremacy and developing military might. As the argument goes, while China adapts itself to the Western-led international order, it is increasingly able to dictate behaviors and international norms according to its preference and its interests.[2] In other words, while expanding its economic influence and military

> **❝** With both elegance and clarity, Kang shows that China's rise has been 'peaceful'—and starkly so when compared to the belligerence that has been endemic to the West since the Middle Ages. China's interest is squarely to ensure that peace and stability remains by and large undisturbed. The odds are good: reasoning that there is more to be gained from accommodation than from balancing and confrontation, countries in East and Southeast Asia have come to accept China's rise. **❞**
>
> Jalal Alamgir, "Applied Constructivism Rising"

power, China is making the region, and to some extent the international order, more similar to itself and more suitable to its leading role. Consequently, it appears as though the potential link between Chinese integration and "sinicization" will be an important topic for foreign-policy analysts and international relations scholars in the coming years.

This kind of research has been influenced by, among others, David C. Kang and by his ideas, particularly the fact that China's rise entails a return to a Sinocentric* order, in which China would be able to shape the institutional and normative structure of international politics in East Asia.

Future Directions

Kang's work has influenced a number of China and East Asia specialists, among them the scholar Robert E. Kelly,* who presents the concept of Confucian* peace as a cornerstone of Asian identity, and integral to the political and economic stability Asia enjoyed before Western colonization of the region.[3] Clear traces of Kang's approach appear in the political scientist Allen Carlson's* research, in which he analyzed the influence of Sinocentrism and its ancient predecessor Tianxia*—the idea that China was the center of the world, and all other peoples were barbarians—on China's foreign policy toward the Asia Pacific region.[4]

Other authors have followed Kang's forecast of the possible return of a Sinocentric system in Asia, including William A. Callahan,* whose work centers on the Chinese discourses that seek to legitimize China's political and economic leadership in Asia,[5] and Linsay Cunningham-Cross's* research on how Chinese elites rely on historical, imperialist discourses to justify its current policies.[6]

Kang's work has played a central role in reactivating the debate about the concept of Sinocentrism. Several scholars, such as the scholar of Asian identity Gilbert Rozman* and the international relations scholar Zhang Feng,* have studied this phenomenon in relation to Asian international affairs. Both Rozman and Feng, however, have presented a quite different interpretation of the concept and its consequences. According to Kang, the Chinese idea of the tributary system,* and the broad acceptance of the return of Chinese centrality, if not superiority, is legitimized by Asian historical and cultural legacies. By contrast, Rozman argues that this narrative was largely created by the Chinese elites, who have a vested interest in appearing to be a welcomed leader, amicably situated at the center of Asia and promoting Confucian harmony.[7]

Rozman sees China using this narrative of legitimacy to spread its influence in the region and replace its past communist* ideology, which, in the post-Cold War* era, is no longer convincing. Whereas Kang portrays Sinocentrism as something inherently positive, Rozman represents it as a defensive political response to China's crisis of legitimacy among some countries in the region.

Summary

China Rising is widely considered a seminal text in contemporary international relations. It has affected what is arguably the most important debate in twenty-first-century global politics: the rise of China and its consequences. Kang's ideas and assessment of China's rise have contributed to building a poignant and credible alternative perspective on current East Asian international politics, Sino-American relations, and the future of Chinese foreign policy. A great many academics and practitioners, especially in the United States, perceive China as a catalyst for instability and a direct challenge to American global leadership.[8] Consequently, they promote an approach aimed at curtailing the expansion of Chinese influence and power in East Asia. Kang highlights how this approach could be detrimental for the stability and development of the region and counterproductive for the United States. A confrontational stance toward China could incite a political crisis between Asian states and Washington, further accelerating the demise of American leadership in Asia.[9]

Kang's ideas are relevant and influential because they convincingly oppose the mainstream Western position, both in theory and in the realm of policy-making. While realism* assumes concepts such as anarchy,* balance of power,* and the competitive nature of power politics as universal, Kang stresses the uniqueness of Asian history, the particular history of regional hierarchy,* the role of shared identity, and the legitimacy and the inclusiveness of the Asian institutional and cultural political tradition.

Kang's work succeeds in framing a solid, theoretically grounded critique of the current American intellectual and strategic approach to Asia, highlighting the possible drawbacks of its policies aimed at competing politically, economically, and militarily for dominance in East Asia.

NOTES

1   Ann Kent, "China's International Socialization: The Role of International Organizations," *Global Governance* 8, no. 3 (2002): 343–64; G. John Ikenberry, "The Rise of China and the Future of the West: Can the Liberal System Survive?" *Foreign Affairs* 87, no. 1 (2008): 23–37; Quddus Z. Snyder, "The Illiberal Trading State: Liberal Systemic Theory and the Mechanism of Socialization," *Journal of Peace Research* 50, no. 1 (2013): 33–45; Alastair I. Johnston, *Social States: China in International Institutions*, 1980–2000 (Princeton, NJ: Princeton University Press, 2008).

2   Peter J. Katzenstein (ed.), *Sinicization and the Rise of China: Civilizational Processes beyond East and West* (Abingdon: Routledge, 2012); Allen Carlson, "Moving beyond Sovereignty? A Brief Consideration of Recent Changes in China's Approach to International Order and the Emergence of the Tianxia Concept," *Journal of Contemporary China* 20, no. 68 (2011): 89–102; Gregory Chin and Ramesh Thakur, "Will China Change the Rules of Global Order?" *The Washington Quarterly* 33, no. 4 (2010): 119–38.

3   Robert E. Kelly, "A 'Confucian Long Peace' in Pre-Western East Asia?" *European Journal of International Relations* 18, no. 3 (2012): 407–30.

4   Carlson, "Moving beyond Sovereignty?"

5   William A. Callahan, "Chinese Visions of World Order: Post-Hegemonic or a New Hegemony?" *International Studies Review* 10, no. 4 (2008): 749–61.

6   Linsay Cunningham-Cross, "Using the Past to (Re)Write the Future: Yan Xuetong, Pre-Qin Thought and China's Rise to Power," *China Information* 26, no. 2 (2012): 219–33.

7   Gilbert Rozman, "Invocations of Chinese Traditions in International Relations," *Journal of Chinese Political Science* 17, no. 2 (2012): 111–24.

8   Robert S. Ross, "US Grand Strategy, the Rise of China, and US National Security Strategy for East Asia," *Strategic Studies Quarterly* 7, no. 2 (2013): 20–40; Aaron L. Friedberg, *A Contest for Supremacy: China, America, and the Struggle for Mastery in Asia* (New York: W. W. Norton & Company, 2011).

9   David C. Kang, "Is America Listening to Its East Asian Allies? Hugh White's *The China Choice*," *Pac Net* 64 (2012): 1–4.

GLOSSARY

GLOSSARY OF TERMS

Analytical eclecticism: this analytical approach in the social sciences uses multiple theories rather than relying on one theory or a fixed set of assumptions.

Anarchy: the absence of an authority higher than sovereign states in the form of a universally recognized world government, or global watchdog.

Asian financial crisis: a major financial crisis in East Asia that occurred from July 1997 to January 1998.

Balance of power theory: the tendency of sovereign nations to take action, such as forming alliances, to limit the disproportional power of a single state.

Balance of threat theory: the claim that states do not balance against power but instead against a threat—a nearby state with significant military capabilities that is perceived as willing to attack.

Bandwagoning: a strategy adopted by a weaker state that aligns itself with a stronger power or with the state that represents a threat to its security.

Cold War (1946–89): a period of tension between the Western bloc (America and its allies) and the Eastern bloc (the Soviet Union and its allies). While the US and Soviet Union never engaged in direct military conflict, they engaged in covert and proxy wars and espionage against one another.

Communism: a political and economic system based on the public ownership of a country's resources and industry, and the equitable distribution of wealth among its citizens, where social class has been abolished.

Confucian: pertaining to the system of morality and ethics established by the ancient Chinese philosopher Confucius (551–479 B.C.E.), whose teachings focused on cultivating harmonious relations through loyalty, and respect for one's family, ancestors, and social betters, and an overall understanding of one's place in the natural order.

Constructivism: a theory that argues that international relations are shaped by shared ideas and identities. States behave according to their perception of themselves and the other states, which they may consider as friends, rivals, or enemies.

Containment: a strategy of thwarting the rise of a great power through alliances and a balance of power.

Deterrence theory: the theory that nuclear weapons prevent another nuclear state from attacking because of the potential consequences for both sides.

Economic interdependence: an idea of the liberal theory of international relations that commercial trade and dependence between nations will prevent war.

Ethnocentric: focusing on one nation or culture to the exclusion of others.

Eurocentric: perspective focused through a lens of European or Western history and culture to the exclusion of a wider view of the world.

Hegemony: the leadership or dominance of one country over others.

Hierarchy: a vertical system of organization which arranges people, objects, or entities by importance or status.

Liberalism: in international relations, the belief that if nations cooperate, trade, and depend on each other economically, war will be avoided. It also places an important emphasis on international institutions, which it argues are essential to preventing conflict between states.

Napoleonic France: the empire of Napoleon Bonaparte and the dominant power in much of continental Europe in the early nineteenth century.

Nation state: a sovereign state based on the idea of a common nation or culture.

Nazi Germany: a period of German history from 1933 to 1945 under the leadership of Adolf Hitler's extremely right-wing Nazi Party.

Neorealism: also known as structural realism, this is an approach to international relations theory first proposed by Kenneth N. Waltz. While maintaining the basic tenets of the realist tradition, such as the adversarial nature of politics, it dismisses the role of human nature, and focuses on the role of international structures and material factors.

9/11: the name given to a series of terrorist attacks on New York and Washington DC on September 11, 2001. The attacks, orchestrated by militant Islamist group Al Qaeda, killed around 3,000 people.

Positive-sum game: a notion that all players gain from an interaction or policy in international relations.

Positivism: a theory that claims that a social fact can be known through external observation. From observation it is possible to deduce laws. The main aim of social science is, therefore, to derive laws or attempt to reveal accepted laws to be false through new observations.

Rationalism: a theory that claims that decisions to act are made on a rational basis based on ordered preferences, and focusing on the most cost-effective means to achieve a specific objective.

Realism: the belief that states seek to maintain or expand power and security in a state of anarchy in international relations. Realists see competition and conflict as largely unavoidable.

Revisionist power: states that are willing to overthrow the international order. To do so, they might act aggressively against the current hegemon (dominant power). Examples of revisionist powers are Germany and Japan before World War II and Napoleonic France.

Sinicization: a theory stating that, through international relations, China is diffusing its identity and vision of the world, and transforming the regional and global order.

Sinocentric system: a hierarchical order that characterized East Asia from the eleventh to the nineteenth centuries. The Chinese emperor was considered the only legitimate ruler of the entire world; other kings derived their authority from the emperor and recognized his superiority by offering tributes to him.

Sovereignty: the authority of a state to govern itself without any outside interference.

Soviet Union: the Union of Soviet Socialist Republics (USSR) was a Eurasian empire that arose from the Russian Revolution in 1917, and that consisted of Russia and 14 satellite states in Eastern Europe, the Baltic and Black Seas, and Central Asia, existing from 1922 to 1991.

Taiwan Strait Crisis: a series of twentieth-century conflicts between the People's Republic of China and Taiwan over disputed territory.

Tianxia: in ancient China, the idea that China was the center of the world, and all other peoples were barbarians.

Tributary system: a system from the eleventh to the nineteenth centuries, under which kings from other Asian nations paid tributes to the Chinese emperor out of respect and in exchange for peace and security.

War on terror: an ongoing period of Western war aimed at containing the threat of terrorism following the September 11, 2001 attacks in the United States.

Westphalian sovereignty: a form of nation-state authority that guarantees that the legitimate ruler of a country can exercise exclusive power over their territory and population, free from external interference. This concept, which recognizes European states as equals, was formalized with the Peace Treaty of Westphalia of 1648 (a treaty signed in the region that ended a long period of European conflict).

World Trade Organization (WTO): an institution based in Switzerland and founded in 1995 to promote international trade. The governments of its 161 member countries can use this forum to negotiate trade agreements and settle trade disputes.

World War I (1914–18): a global conflict centered in Europe in which the Allies (chiefly Britain, France, Italy, Russia, and the United States) defeated the Central Powers (chiefly Germany, Austria-Hungary, and the Ottoman Empire).

World War II (1939–45): a global conflict in which the Allies (chiefly Britain, the United States, and the Soviet Union) defeated the Axis (Germany, Italy, and Japan).

PEOPLE MENTIONED IN THE TEXT

Amitav Acharya (b. 1962) is a professor of international relations at American University in Washington, DC. He is the author of *The Making of Southeast Asia* (2013) and *The End of American World Order* (2014).

Richard Betts (b. 1947) is a professor of political science at Columbia University, and the author of *Enemies of Intelligence: Knowledge and Power in American National Security* (2007). His areas of expertise include international conflict, US foreign policy, and terrorism.

Napoleon Bonaparte (1769–1821) was emperor of France for a decade starting in 1804 and waged a series of successful military campaigns throughout Europe, winning domination over much of the continent until his defeat in 1815 at the Battle of Waterloo.

George W. Bush (b. 1946) was the 43rd president of the United States. He was in office from 2001 to 2009.

Barry Buzan (b. 1946) is emeritus professor of international relations at the London School of Economics and Political Science. He is the author of many important works, and co-edited *Non-Western International Relations Theory: Perspectives on and beyond Asia* (2010).

William A. Callahan is professor of international politics and China studies in the politics department at the University of Manchester and co-director of the British Inter-University China Centre (BICC).

Allen Carlson is associate professor of government at Cornell University and a scholar of Chinese politics, foreign policy, and Asian security. He is the author of *Unifying China, Integrating with the World: Securing Chinese Sovereignty in the Reform Era (2005), among other important works.*

Steve Chan (b. 1976) is a professor of political science at the University of Colorado, Boulder and a prolific author on the subject of Asian International Relations.

Ta-Tuan Ch'en was a scholar on Chinese politics and foreign policy. He published several important works, including *The Chinese World Order* (1968).

Bill Clinton (b. 1946) was the 42nd president of the United States. He was in office from 1993 to 2001.

Linsay Cunningham-Cross is a specialist in international relations and Asian history and politics.

Reinhard Drifte is emeritus professor of Japanese politics at the University of Newcastle. His research focuses on Japan's foreign and security policy, and security issues in Northeast Asia.

John K. Fairbank (1907–91) was a scholar of Chinese history and Chinese–American relations. He wrote several important works including *China: A New History* (1992).

Zhang Feng is a fellow of international relations at Australian National University. He has authored several important works, including *Chinese Hegemony: Grand Strategy and International Institutions in East Asian History* (2015).

Stefan Fergus is a journalist who writes about US–Chinese relations.

Evelyn Goh is Shedden Professor of Strategic Policy Studies at the Australian National University and a scholar of international relations in the Asia-Pacific region. She is the author of *The Struggle for Order: Hegemony, Hierarchy and Transition in Post-Cold War East Asia* (2013), among other important works.

Adolf Hitler (1889–1945) was the leader of Nazi Germany from 1933 to 1945. His regime was responsible for initiating World War II and for the Holocaust.

Robert E. Kelly is associate professor of international relations at Pusan National University in South Korea and a scholar of US foreign policy and security in Asia. He is the author of a number of articles including "The 'Pivot' and Its Problems: American Foreign Policy in Northeast Asia" (2014), and is a contributor to the Economist Intelligence Unit.

John Mearsheimer (b. 1947) is professor of political science at the University of Chicago. He is the author of *The Tragedy of Great Power Politics* (2001), among numerous other important works.

Barack Obama (b. 1961) is the 44th president of the United States. His foreign-policy approach to China has been characterized by a mixture of cooperation and containment.

Gilbert Rozman is Musgrave Professor of Sociology at Princeton University, and a scholar of Asian identity and international relations. He is the author of a number of books and articles, including *The East Asian Region: Confucian Heritage and Its Modern Adaptation* (1991).

Peter Van Ness is a visiting fellow at Australian National University, College of Asia and the Pacific. He is the author of important works on China, including *Revolution and Chinese Foreign Policy* (1970).

Stephen Walt (b. 1955) is professor of international relations at Harvard University and a neorealist. In a journal article titled "Alliance Formation and the Balance of World Power" (1985), he expanded the concept of "balance of power" to take account of state identities, calling it "balance of threat."

Kenneth Waltz (1924–2013) was a key international relations scholar. The author of *Theory of International Politics* (1979), he is considered the founder of the neorealist approach to international relations. He also wrote *Man, the State, and War* (1959), in which he discussed three levels of analysis in the study of international politics: individual, state, and international system.

Alexander Wendt (b. 1958) is Ralph D. Mershon Professor of International Security at Ohio State University, and the author of *Social Theory of International Politics* (1999). He is a major proponent of constructivism, one of the key theoretical approaches to the study of international politics.

William Wohlforth (b. 1959) is Daniel Webster Professor of Government at Dartmouth College. He is a neorealist scholar of international relations, and the author of *America Abroad: the United States' Global Role in the Twenty-First Century* (forthcoming), among other important works.

WORKS CITED

WORKS CITED

Acharya, Amitav. *Whose Ideas Matter? Agency and Power in Asian Regionalism.* Ithaca, NY: Cornell University Press, 2009.

"Will Asia's Past Be Its Future?" *International Security* 28, no. 3 (2003): 149–64.

Acharya, Amitav, and Barry Buzan. "Why Is There No Non-Western International Relations Theory? An Introduction." *International Relations of the Asia-Pacific* 7, no. 3 (2007): 287–312.

Aggarwal, Vinod K., and Sara A. Newland, eds. *Responding to China's Rise: US and EU Strategies*. New York: Springer, 2015.

Alamgir, Jalal. "Applied Constructivism Rising." *Asia Policy* 6 (2008): 162–5.

Betts, Richard K. "Wealth, Power, and Instability: East Asia and the United States after the Cold War." *International Security* 18, no. 3 (1993): 34–77.

Broomfield, Emma V. "Perceptions of Danger: The China Threat Theory." *Journal of Contemporary China* 12, no. 35 (2003): 265–84.

Callahan, William A. "Chinese Visions of World Order: Post-Hegemonic or a New Hegemony?" *International Studies Review* 10, no. 4 (2008): 749–61.

Carlson, Allen. "Moving beyond Sovereignty? A Brief Consideration of Recent Changes in China's Approach to International Order and the Emergence of the Tianxia Concept." *Journal of Contemporary China* 20, no. 68 (2011): 89–102.

Cha, Victor D., and David C. Kang. "Complex Patchworks: US Alliances as Part of Asia's Regional Architecture." *Asia Policy* 11 (2011): 27–50.

Nuclear North Korea: A Debate on Engagement Strategies. New York: Columbia University Press, 2003.

Chan, Steve. "An Odd Thing Happened on the Way to Balancing: East Asian States' Reactions to China's Rise." *International Studies Review* 12, no. 3 (2010): 387–412.

Chin, Gregory, and Ramesh Thakur. "Will China Change the Rules of Global Order?" *The Washington Quarterly* 33, no. 4 (2010): 119–38.

Christensen, Thomas J. "Fostering Stability or Creating a Monster? The Rise of China and US Policy toward East Asia." *International Security* 31, no. 1 (2006): 81–126.

Worse than a Monolith: Alliance Politics and Problems of Coercive Diplomacy in Asia. Princeton, NJ: Princeton University Press, 2011.

Cunningham-Cross, Linsay. "Using the Past to (Re)Write the Future: Yan Xuetong, Pre-Qin Thought and China's Rise to Power." *China Information* 26, no. 2 (2012): 219–33.

Drezner, Daniel W. "Does Obama Have a Grand Strategy? Why We Need Doctrines in Uncertain Times." *Foreign Affairs* 90, no. 4 (2011): 57–62.

Drifte, Reinhard. *Japan's Security Relations with China since 1989: From Balancing to Bandwagoning?* Abingdon: Routledge, 2012.

Economy, Elizabeth C., and Michel Oksenberg. *China Joins the World: Progress and Prospects*. New York: Council on Foreign Relations, 1999.

Fairbank, John King, and Ta-tuan Ch'en. *The Chinese World Order: Traditional China's Foreign Relations*. Cambridge, MA: Harvard University Press, 1968.

Ferguson, Niall, and Moritz Schularick. "'Chimerica' and the Global Asset Market Boom." *International Finance* 10, no. 3 (2007): 215–39.

Fravel, M. Taylor. "Regime Insecurity and International Cooperation: Explaining China's Compromises in Territorial Disputes." *International Security* 30, no. 2 (2005): 46–83.

Friedberg, Aaron L. *A Contest for Supremacy: China, America, and the Struggle for Mastery in Asia*. New York: W. W. Norton & Company, 2011.

"Ripe for Rivalry: Prospects for Peace in a Multipolar Asia." *International Security* 18, no. 3 (1993): 5–33.

Frost, Ellen L. "Shifting the Burden of Proof." *Asia Policy* 6 (2008): 153–7.

George, Alexander L., and Richard Smoke. "Deterrence and Foreign Policy." *World Politics* 41, no. 2 (1989): 170–82.

Glaser, Bonnie S. "Pivot to Asia: Prepare for Unintended Consequences." In *2012 Global Forecast, Risk, Opportunity and the Next Administration*, edited by Craig Cohen and Josiane Gabel, 22–4. Washington, DC: Center for Strategic and International Studies, 2012.

Goh, Evelyn. "Power, Interest, and Identity: Reviving the Sinocentric Hierarchy in East Asia." *Asia Policy* 6 (2008): 148–53.

"The United States in Asia: Reflections on Deterrence, Alliances, and the 'Balance' of Power." *International Relations of the Asia-Pacific* 12, no. 3 (2012): 511–18.

Hamashita, Takeshi. *China, East Asia and the Global Economy: Regional and Historical Perspectives*. Abingdon: Routledge, 2013.

Hughes, Christopher W. *Japan's Remilitarisation*. Abingdon: Routledge for International Institute for Strategic Studies, 2009.

Ikenberry, G. John. "Power and Liberal Order: America's Postwar World Order in Transition." *International Relations of the Asia-Pacific* 5, no. 2 (2005): 133–52.

"The Rise of China and the Future of the West: Can the Liberal System Survive?" *Foreign Affairs* 87, no. 1 (2008): 23–37.

Johnston, Alastair Iain. "Is China a Status Quo Power?" *International Security* 27, no. 4 (2003): 5–56.

Social States: China in International Institutions, 1980–2000. Princeton, NJ: Princeton University Press, 2008.

Kang, David C. "Authority and Legitimacy in International Relations: Evidence from Korean and Japanese Relations in Pre-modern East Asia." *The Chinese Journal of International Politics* 5, no. 1 (2012): 55–71.

China Rising: Peace, Power, and Order in East Asia. New York: Columbia University Press, 2007.

Crony Capitalism: Corruption and Development in South Korea and the Philippines. Cambridge: Cambridge University Press, 2002.

East Asia before the West: Five Centuries of Trade and Tribute. New York: Columbia University Press, 2010.

"Getting Asia Wrong: The Need for New Analytical Frameworks." *International Security* 27, no. 4 (2003): 57–85.

"Hierarchy and Legitimacy in International Systems: The Tribute System in Early Modern East Asia." *Security Studies* 19, no. 4 (2010): 591–622.

"Hierarchy, Balancing, and Empirical Puzzles in Asian International Relations." *International Security* 28, no. 3 (2003): 165–80.

"Hierarchy in Asian International Relations: 1300–1900." *Asian Security* 1, no. 1 (2005): 53–79.

"International Relations Theory and East Asian History: An Overview." *Journal of East Asian Studies* 13, no. 2 (2013): 181–205.

"Is America Listening to Its East Asian Allies? Hugh White's *The China Choice*." *Pac Net* 64 (2012): 1–4.

"The Theoretical Roots of Hierarchy in International Relations." *Australian Journal of International Affairs* 58, no. 3 (2004): 337–52.

"Why China's Rise Will Be Peaceful: Hierarchy and Stability in the East Asian Region." *Perspectives on Politics* 3, no. 3 (2005): 551–4.

Katzenstein, Peter J. *Sinicization and the Rise of China: Civilizational Processes beyond East and West*. Abingdon: Routledge, 2012.

Kelly, Robert E. "A 'Confucian Long Peace' in Pre-Western East Asia?" *European Journal of International Relations* 18, no. 3 (2012): 407–30.

Kent, Ann. "China's International Socialization: The Role of International Organizations." *Global Governance* 8, no. 3 (2002): 343–64.

Lanteigne, Marc. *China and International Institutions: Alternate Paths to Global Power*. Abingdon: Routledge, 2005.

Larsen, Kirk W. "Comforting Fictions: The Tribute System, the Westphalian Order, and Sino-Korean Relations." *Journal of East Asian Studies* 13, no. 2 (2013): 233–57.

Larson, Deborah Welch, and Alexei Shevchenko. "Status Seekers: Chinese and Russian Responses to US Primacy." *International Security* 34, no. 4 (2010): 63–95.

Manyin, Mark E. *Pivot to the Pacific? The Obama Administration's "Rebalancing" toward Asia*. Washington, DC: Congressional Research Service, 2012.

Mearsheimer, John J. "China's Unpeaceful Rise." *Current History* 105, no. 690 (2006): 160–2.

The Tragedy of Great Power Politics. New York: W. W. Norton & Company, 2001.

Myers, Ramon Hawley, Michael Oksenberg, and David Shambaugh. *Making China Policy: Lessons from the Bush and Clinton Administrations*. Lanham, MD: Rowman & Littlefield, 2001.

Richardson, James L. "Asia-Pacific: The Case for Geopolitical Optimism." *National Interest* 38 (1994): 28–39.

Ross, Robert S. "The 1995–96 Taiwan Strait Confrontation: Coercion, Credibility, and the Use of Force." *International Security* 25, no. 2 (2000): 87–123.

"The Problem with the Pivot." *Foreign Affairs* 91, no. 6 (2012): 70–82.

"US Grand Strategy, the Rise of China, and US National Security Strategy for East Asia." *Strategic Studies Quarterly* 7, no. 2 (2013): 20–40.

Rozman, Gilbert. "Invocations of Chinese Traditions in International Relations." *Journal of Chinese Political Science* 17, no. 2 (2012): 111–24.

Samuels, Richard J. *Securing Japan: Tokyo's Grand Strategy and the Future of East Asia*. Ithaca, NY: Cornell University Press, 2007.

Schroeder, Paul. "Historical Reality vs. Neo-Realist Theory." *International Security* 19, no. 1 (1994): 108–48.

Shambaugh, David. "Assessing the US Pivot to Asia," *Strategic Studies Quarterly* 7, no. 2 (2013): 10–19.

"Coping with a Conflicted China." *The Washington Quarterly* 34, no. 1 (2011): 7–27.

Sil, Rudra, and Peter Katzenstein. "Analytic Eclecticism in the Study of World Politics: Reconfiguring Problems and Mechanisms across Research Traditions." *Perspectives on Politics* 8, no. 2 (2010): 411–31.

Snyder, Glenn H, *Alliance Politics*. Ithaca, NY: Cornell University Press, 2007.

Snyder, Quddus Z. "The Illiberal Trading State: Liberal Systemic Theory and the Mechanism of Socialization." *Journal of Peace Research* 50, no. 1 (2013): 33–45.

Stefan, Fergus. "Book Review: David C. Kang, *China Rising: Peace, Power, and Order in East Asia*." *East Asia* 26, no. 2 (2009): 163–6.

Swaine, Michael D. "Chinese Leadership and Elite Responses to the US Pacific Pivot." *China Leadership Monitor* 38 (2012): 1–26.

Twomey, Christopher P. "Balancing Identity and Reality." *Asia Policy* 6 (2008): 157–61.

Ueki, Chikako. "The Rise of 'China Threat' Arguments." PhD diss., Massachusetts Institute of Technology, 2006.

Van Ness, Peter. "Anticipating the Unexpected." *Asia Policy* 6 (2008): 168–72.

Walt, Stephen M. "Alliance Formation and the Balance of World Power." *International Security* 9, no. 4 (1985): 3–43.

Waltz, Kenneth N. "The Emerging Structure of International Politics." *International Security* 18, no. 2 (1993): 44–79.

Wendt, Alexander. *Social Theory of International Politics*. Cambridge: Cambridge University Press, 1999.

Yang, Yi Edward, and Xinsheng Liu. "The 'China Threat' through the Lens of US Print Media: 1992–2006." *Journal of Contemporary China* 21, no. 76 (2012): 695–711.

Yee, Herbert. "Introduction." In *China's Rise—Threat or Opportunity?*, edited by Herbert Yee, 1–6. Abingdon: Routledge, 2011.

THE MACAT LIBRARY
BY DISCIPLINE

AFRICANA STUDIES

Chinua Achebe's *An Image of Africa: Racism in Conrad's Heart of Darkness*
W. E. B. Du Bois's *The Souls of Black Folk*
Zora Neale Huston's *Characteristics of Negro Expression*
Martin Luther King Jr's *Why We Can't Wait*
Toni Morrison's *Playing in the Dark: Whiteness in the American Literary Imagination*

ANTHROPOLOGY

Arjun Appadurai's *Modernity at Large: Cultural Dimensions of Globalisation*
Philippe Ariès's *Centuries of Childhood*
Franz Boas's *Race, Language and Culture*
Kim Chan & Renée Mauborgne's *Blue Ocean Strategy*
Jared Diamond's *Guns, Germs & Steel: the Fate of Human Societies*
Jared Diamond's *Collapse: How Societies Choose to Fail or Survive*
E. E. Evans-Pritchard's *Witchcraft, Oracles and Magic Among the Azande*
James Ferguson's *The Anti-Politics Machine*
Clifford Geertz's *The Interpretation of Cultures*
David Graeber's *Debt: the First 5000 Years*
Karen Ho's *Liquidated: An Ethnography of Wall Street*
Geert Hofstede's *Culture's Consequences: Comparing Values, Behaviors, Institutes and Organizations across Nations*
Claude Lévi-Strauss's *Structural Anthropology*
Jay Macleod's *Ain't No Makin' It: Aspirations and Attainment in a Low-Income Neighborhood*
Saba Mahmood's *The Politics of Piety: The Islamic Revival and the Feminist Subject*
Marcel Mauss's *The Gift*

BUSINESS

Jean Lave & Etienne Wenger's *Situated Learning*
Theodore Levitt's *Marketing Myopia*
Burton G. Malkiel's *A Random Walk Down Wall Street*
Douglas McGregor's *The Human Side of Enterprise*
Michael Porter's *Competitive Strategy: Creating and Sustaining Superior Performance*
John Kotter's *Leading Change*
C. K. Prahalad & Gary Hamel's *The Core Competence of the Corporation*

CRIMINOLOGY

Michelle Alexander's *The New Jim Crow: Mass Incarceration in the Age of Colorblindness*
Michael R. Gottfredson & Travis Hirschi's *A General Theory of Crime*
Richard Herrnstein & Charles A. Murray's *The Bell Curve: Intelligence and Class Structure in American Life*
Elizabeth Loftus's *Eyewitness Testimony*
Jay Macleod's *Ain't No Makin' It: Aspirations and Attainment in a Low-Income Neighborhood*
Philip Zimbardo's *The Lucifer Effect*

ECONOMICS

Janet Abu-Lughod's *Before European Hegemony*
Ha-Joon Chang's *Kicking Away the Ladder*
David Brion Davis's *The Problem of Slavery in the Age of Revolution*
Milton Friedman's *The Role of Monetary Policy*
Milton Friedman's *Capitalism and Freedom*
David Graeber's *Debt: the First 5000 Years*
Friedrich Hayek's *The Road to Serfdom*
Karen Ho's *Liquidated: An Ethnography of Wall Street*

John Maynard Keynes's *The General Theory of Employment, Interest and Money*
Charles P. Kindleberger's *Manias, Panics and Crashes*
Robert Lucas's *Why Doesn't Capital Flow from Rich to Poor Countries?*
Burton G. Malkiel's *A Random Walk Down Wall Street*
Thomas Robert Malthus's *An Essay on the Principle of Population*
Karl Marx's *Capital*
Thomas Piketty's *Capital in the Twenty-First Century*
Amartya Sen's *Development as Freedom*
Adam Smith's *The Wealth of Nations*
Nassim Nicholas Taleb's *The Black Swan: The Impact of the Highly Improbable*
Amos Tversky's & Daniel Kahneman's *Judgment under Uncertainty: Heuristics and Biases*
Mahbub Ul Haq's *Reflections on Human Development*
Max Weber's *The Protestant Ethic and the Spirit of Capitalism*

FEMINISM AND GENDER STUDIES

Judith Butler's *Gender Trouble*
Simone De Beauvoir's *The Second Sex*
Michel Foucault's *History of Sexuality*
Betty Friedan's *The Feminine Mystique*
Saba Mahmood's *The Politics of Piety: The Islamic Revival and the Feminist Subject*
Joan Wallach Scott's *Gender and the Politics of History*
Mary Wollstonecraft's *A Vindication of the Rights of Woman*
Virginia Woolf's *A Room of One's Own*

GEOGRAPHY

The Brundtland Report's *Our Common Future*
Rachel Carson's *Silent Spring*
Charles Darwin's *On the Origin of Species*
James Ferguson's *The Anti-Politics Machine*
Jane Jacobs's *The Death and Life of Great American Cities*
James Lovelock's *Gaia: A New Look at Life on Earth*
Amartya Sen's *Development as Freedom*
Mathis Wackernagel & William Rees's *Our Ecological Footprint*

HISTORY

Janet Abu-Lughod's *Before European Hegemony*
Benedict Anderson's *Imagined Communities*
Bernard Bailyn's *The Ideological Origins of the American Revolution*
Hanna Batatu's *The Old Social Classes And The Revolutionary Movements Of Iraq*
Christopher Browning's *Ordinary Men: Reserve Police Batallion 101 and the Final Solution in Poland*
Edmund Burke's *Reflections on the Revolution in France*
William Cronon's *Nature's Metropolis: Chicago And The Great West*
Alfred W. Crosby's *The Columbian Exchange*
Hamid Dabashi's *Iran: A People Interrupted*
David Brion Davis's *The Problem of Slavery in the Age of Revolution*
Nathalie Zemon Davis's *The Return of Martin Guerre*
Jared Diamond's *Guns, Germs & Steel: the Fate of Human Societies*
Frank Dikotter's *Mao's Great Famine*
John W Dower's *War Without Mercy: Race And Power In The Pacific War*
W. E. B. Du Bois's *The Souls of Black Folk*
Richard J. Evans's *In Defence of History*
Lucien Febvre's *The Problem of Unbelief in the 16th Century*
Sheila Fitzpatrick's *Everyday Stalinism*

Eric Foner's *Reconstruction: America's Unfinished Revolution, 1863-1877*
Michel Foucault's *Discipline and Punish*
Michel Foucault's *History of Sexuality*
Francis Fukuyama's *The End of History and the Last Man*
John Lewis Gaddis's *We Now Know: Rethinking Cold War History*
Ernest Gellner's *Nations and Nationalism*
Eugene Genovese's *Roll, Jordan, Roll: The World the Slaves Made*
Carlo Ginzburg's *The Night Battles*
Daniel Goldhagen's *Hitler's Willing Executioners*
Jack Goldstone's *Revolution and Rebellion in the Early Modern World*
Antonio Gramsci's *The Prison Notebooks*
Alexander Hamilton, John Jay & James Madison's *The Federalist Papers*
Christopher Hill's *The World Turned Upside Down*
Carole Hillenbrand's *The Crusades: Islamic Perspectives*
Thomas Hobbes's *Leviathan*
Eric Hobsbawm's *The Age Of Revolution*
John A. Hobson's *Imperialism: A Study*
Albert Hourani's *History of the Arab Peoples*
Samuel P. Huntington's *The Clash of Civilizations and the Remaking of World Order*
C. L. R. James's *The Black Jacobins*
Tony Judt's *Postwar: A History of Europe Since 1945*
Ernst Kantorowicz's *The King's Two Bodies: A Study in Medieval Political Theology*
Paul Kennedy's *The Rise and Fall of the Great Powers*
Ian Kershaw's *The "Hitler Myth": Image and Reality in the Third Reich*
John Maynard Keynes's *The General Theory of Employment, Interest and Money*
Charles P. Kindleberger's *Manias, Panics and Crashes*
Martin Luther King Jr's *Why We Can't Wait*
Henry Kissinger's *World Order: Reflections on the Character of Nations and the Course of History*
Thomas Kuhn's *The Structure of Scientific Revolutions*
Georges Lefebvre's *The Coming of the French Revolution*
John Locke's *Two Treatises of Government*
Niccolò Machiavelli's *The Prince*
Thomas Robert Malthus's *An Essay on the Principle of Population*
Mahmood Mamdani's *Citizen and Subject: Contemporary Africa And The Legacy Of Late Colonialism*
Karl Marx's *Capital*
Stanley Milgram's *Obedience to Authority*
John Stuart Mill's *On Liberty*
Thomas Paine's *Common Sense*
Thomas Paine's *Rights of Man*
Geoffrey Parker's *Global Crisis: War, Climate Change and Catastrophe in the Seventeenth Century*
Jonathan Riley-Smith's *The First Crusade and the Idea of Crusading*
Jean-Jacques Rousseau's *The Social Contract*
Joan Wallach Scott's *Gender and the Politics of History*
Theda Skocpol's *States and Social Revolutions*
Adam Smith's *The Wealth of Nations*
Timothy Snyder's *Bloodlands: Europe Between Hitler and Stalin*
Sun Tzu's *The Art of War*
Keith Thomas's *Religion and the Decline of Magic*
Thucydides's *The History of the Peloponnesian War*
Frederick Jackson Turner's *The Significance of the Frontier in American History*
Odd Arne Westad's *The Global Cold War: Third World Interventions And The Making Of Our Times*

LITERATURE

Chinua Achebe's *An Image of Africa: Racism in Conrad's Heart of Darkness*
Roland Barthes's *Mythologies*
Homi K. Bhabha's *The Location of Culture*
Judith Butler's *Gender Trouble*
Simone De Beauvoir's *The Second Sex*
Ferdinand De Saussure's *Course in General Linguistics*
T. S. Eliot's *The Sacred Wood: Essays on Poetry and Criticism*
Zora Neale Huston's *Characteristics of Negro Expression*
Toni Morrison's *Playing in the Dark: Whiteness in the American Literary Imagination*
Edward Said's *Orientalism*
Gayatri Chakravorty Spivak's *Can the Subaltern Speak?*
Mary Wollstonecraft's *A Vindication of the Rights of Women*
Virginia Woolf's *A Room of One's Own*

PHILOSOPHY

Elizabeth Anscombe's *Modern Moral Philosophy*
Hannah Arendt's *The Human Condition*
Aristotle's *Metaphysics*
Aristotle's *Nicomachean Ethics*
Edmund Gettier's *Is Justified True Belief Knowledge?*
Georg Wilhelm Friedrich Hegel's *Phenomenology of Spirit*
David Hume's *Dialogues Concerning Natural Religion*
David Hume's *The Enquiry for Human Understanding*
Immanuel Kant's *Religion within the Boundaries of Mere Reason*
Immanuel Kant's *Critique of Pure Reason*
Søren Kierkegaard's *The Sickness Unto Death*
Søren Kierkegaard's *Fear and Trembling*
C. S. Lewis's *The Abolition of Man*
Alasdair MacIntyre's *After Virtue*
Marcus Aurelius's *Meditations*
Friedrich Nietzsche's *On the Genealogy of Morality*
Friedrich Nietzsche's *Beyond Good and Evil*
Plato's *Republic*
Plato's *Symposium*
Jean-Jacques Rousseau's *The Social Contract*
Gilbert Ryle's *The Concept of Mind*
Baruch Spinoza's *Ethics*
Sun Tzu's *The Art of War*
Ludwig Wittgenstein's *Philosophical Investigations*

POLITICS

Benedict Anderson's *Imagined Communities*
Aristotle's *Politics*
Bernard Bailyn's *The Ideological Origins of the American Revolution*
Edmund Burke's *Reflections on the Revolution in France*
John C. Calhoun's *A Disquisition on Government*
Ha-Joon Chang's *Kicking Away the Ladder*
Hamid Dabashi's *Iran: A People Interrupted*
Hamid Dabashi's *Theology of Discontent: The Ideological Foundation of the Islamic Revolution in Iran*
Robert Dahl's *Democracy and its Critics*
Robert Dahl's *Who Governs?*
David Brion Davis's *The Problem of Slavery in the Age of Revolution*

Alexis De Tocqueville's *Democracy in America*
James Ferguson's *The Anti-Politics Machine*
Frank Dikotter's *Mao's Great Famine*
Sheila Fitzpatrick's *Everyday Stalinism*
Eric Foner's *Reconstruction: America's Unfinished Revolution, 1863-1877*
Milton Friedman's *Capitalism and Freedom*
Francis Fukuyama's *The End of History and the Last Man*
John Lewis Gaddis's *We Now Know: Rethinking Cold War History*
Ernest Gellner's *Nations and Nationalism*
David Graeber's *Debt: the First 5000 Years*
Antonio Gramsci's *The Prison Notebooks*
Alexander Hamilton, John Jay & James Madison's *The Federalist Papers*
Friedrich Hayek's *The Road to Serfdom*
Christopher Hill's *The World Turned Upside Down*
Thomas Hobbes's *Leviathan*
John A. Hobson's *Imperialism: A Study*
Samuel P. Huntington's *The Clash of Civilizations and the Remaking of World Order*
Tony Judt's *Postwar: A History of Europe Since 1945*
David C. Kang's *China Rising: Peace, Power and Order in East Asia*
Paul Kennedy's *The Rise and Fall of Great Powers*
Robert Keohane's *After Hegemony*
Martin Luther King Jr.'s *Why We Can't Wait*
Henry Kissinger's *World Order: Reflections on the Character of Nations and the Course of History*
John Locke's *Two Treatises of Government*
Niccolò Machiavelli's *The Prince*
Thomas Robert Malthus's *An Essay on the Principle of Population*
Mahmood Mamdani's *Citizen and Subject: Contemporary Africa And The Legacy Of Late Colonialism*
Karl Marx's *Capital*
John Stuart Mill's *On Liberty*
John Stuart Mill's *Utilitarianism*
Hans Morgenthau's *Politics Among Nations*
Thomas Paine's *Common Sense*
Thomas Paine's *Rights of Man*
Thomas Piketty's *Capital in the Twenty-First Century*
Robert D. Putman's *Bowling Alone*
John Rawls's *Theory of Justice*
Jean-Jacques Rousseau's *The Social Contract*
Theda Skocpol's *States and Social Revolutions*
Adam Smith's *The Wealth of Nations*
Sun Tzu's *The Art of War*
Henry David Thoreau's *Civil Disobedience*
Thucydides's *The History of the Peloponnesian War*
Kenneth Waltz's *Theory of International Politics*
Max Weber's *Politics as a Vocation*
Odd Arne Westad's *The Global Cold War: Third World Interventions And The Making Of Our Times*

POSTCOLONIAL STUDIES

Roland Barthes's *Mythologies*
Frantz Fanon's *Black Skin, White Masks*
Homi K. Bhabha's *The Location of Culture*
Gustavo Gutiérrez's *A Theology of Liberation*
Edward Said's *Orientalism*
Gayatri Chakravorty Spivak's *Can the Subaltern Speak?*

PSYCHOLOGY

Gordon Allport's *The Nature of Prejudice*
Alan Baddeley & Graham Hitch's *Aggression: A Social Learning Analysis*
Albert Bandura's *Aggression: A Social Learning Analysis*
Leon Festinger's *A Theory of Cognitive Dissonance*
Sigmund Freud's *The Interpretation of Dreams*
Betty Friedan's *The Feminine Mystique*
Michael R. Gottfredson & Travis Hirschi's *A General Theory of Crime*
Eric Hoffer's *The True Believer: Thoughts on the Nature of Mass Movements*
William James's *Principles of Psychology*
Elizabeth Loftus's *Eyewitness Testimony*
A. H. Maslow's *A Theory of Human Motivation*
Stanley Milgram's *Obedience to Authority*
Steven Pinker's *The Better Angels of Our Nature*
Oliver Sacks's *The Man Who Mistook His Wife For a Hat*
Richard Thaler & Cass Sunstein's *Nudge: Improving Decisions About Health, Wealth and Happiness*
Amos Tversky's *Judgment under Uncertainty: Heuristics and Biases*
Philip Zimbardo's *The Lucifer Effect*

SCIENCE

Rachel Carson's *Silent Spring*
William Cronon's *Nature's Metropolis: Chicago And The Great West*
Alfred W. Crosby's *The Columbian Exchange*
Charles Darwin's *On the Origin of Species*
Richard Dawkin's *The Selfish Gene*
Thomas Kuhn's *The Structure of Scientific Revolutions*
Geoffrey Parker's *Global Crisis: War, Climate Change and Catastrophe in the Seventeenth Century*
Mathis Wackernagel & William Rees's *Our Ecological Footprint*

SOCIOLOGY

Michelle Alexander's *The New Jim Crow: Mass Incarceration in the Age of Colorblindness*
Gordon Allport's *The Nature of Prejudice*
Albert Bandura's *Aggression: A Social Learning Analysis*
Hanna Batatu's *The Old Social Classes And The Revolutionary Movements Of Iraq*
Ha-Joon Chang's *Kicking Away the Ladder*
W. E. B. Du Bois's *The Souls of Black Folk*
Émile Durkheim's *On Suicide*
Frantz Fanon's *Black Skin, White Masks*
Frantz Fanon's *The Wretched of the Earth*
Eric Foner's *Reconstruction: America's Unfinished Revolution, 1863-1877*
Eugene Genovese's *Roll, Jordan, Roll: The World the Slaves Made*
Jack Goldstone's *Revolution and Rebellion in the Early Modern World*
Antonio Gramsci's *The Prison Notebooks*
Richard Herrnstein & Charles A Murray's *The Bell Curve: Intelligence and Class Structure in American Life*
Eric Hoffer's *The True Believer: Thoughts on the Nature of Mass Movements*
Jane Jacobs's *The Death and Life of Great American Cities*
Robert Lucas's *Why Doesn't Capital Flow from Rich to Poor Countries?*
Jay Macleod's *Ain't No Makin' It: Aspirations and Attainment in a Low Income Neighborhood*
Elaine May's *Homeward Bound: American Families in the Cold War Era*
Douglas McGregor's *The Human Side of Enterprise*
C. Wright Mills's *The Sociological Imagination*

The Macat Library By Discipline

Thomas Piketty's *Capital in the Twenty-First Century*
Robert D. Putman's *Bowling Alone*
David Riesman's *The Lonely Crowd: A Study of the Changing American Character*
Edward Said's *Orientalism*
Joan Wallach Scott's *Gender and the Politics of History*
Theda Skocpol's *States and Social Revolutions*
Max Weber's *The Protestant Ethic and the Spirit of Capitalism*

THEOLOGY

Augustine's *Confessions*
Benedict's *Rule of St Benedict*
Gustavo Gutiérrez's *A Theology of Liberation*
Carole Hillenbrand's *The Crusades: Islamic Perspectives*
David Hume's *Dialogues Concerning Natural Religion*
Immanuel Kant's *Religion within the Boundaries of Mere Reason*
Ernst Kantorowicz's *The King's Two Bodies: A Study in Medieval Political Theology*
Søren Kierkegaard's *The Sickness Unto Death*
C. S. Lewis's *The Abolition of Man*
Saba Mahmood's *The Politics of Piety: The Islamic Revival and the Feminist Subject*
Baruch Spinoza's *Ethics*
Keith Thomas's *Religion and the Decline of Magic*

COMING SOON

Chris Argyris's *The Individual and the Organisation*
Seyla Benhabib's *The Rights of Others*
Walter Benjamin's *The Work Of Art in the Age of Mechanical Reproduction*
John Berger's *Ways of Seeing*
Pierre Bourdieu's *Outline of a Theory of Practice*
Mary Douglas's *Purity and Danger*
Roland Dworkin's *Taking Rights Seriously*
James G. March's *Exploration and Exploitation in Organisational Learning*
Ikujiro Nonaka's *A Dynamic Theory of Organizational Knowledge Creation*
Griselda Pollock's *Vision and Difference*
Amartya Sen's *Inequality Re-Examined*
Susan Sontag's *On Photography*
Yasser Tabbaa's *The Transformation of Islamic Art*
Ludwig von Mises's *Theory of Money and Credit*

Macat Disciplines

Access the greatest ideas and thinkers across entire disciplines, including

Postcolonial Studies

Roland Barthes's *Mythologies*
Frantz Fanon's *Black Skin, White Masks*
Homi K. Bhabha's *The Location of Culture*
Gustavo Gutiérrez's *A Theology of Liberation*
Edward Said's *Orientalism*
Gayatri Chakravorty Spivak's *Can the Subaltern Speak?*

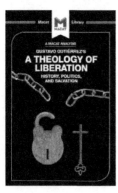

Macat analyses are available from all good bookshops and libraries.

Access hundreds of analyses through one, multimedia tool.
Join free for one month **library.macat.com**

Macat Disciplines

Access the greatest ideas and thinkers across entire disciplines, including

AFRICANA STUDIES

Chinua Achebe's *An Image of Africa: Racism in Conrad's Heart of Darkness*

W. E. B. Du Bois's *The Souls of Black Folk*

Zora Neale Hurston's *Characteristics of Negro Expression*

Martin Luther King Jr.'s *Why We Can't Wait*

Toni Morrison's *Playing in the Dark: Whiteness in the American Literary Imagination*

Macat analyses are available from all good bookshops and libraries.

Access hundreds of analyses through one, multimedia tool.
Join free for one month **library.macat.com**

Macat Disciplines

Access the greatest ideas and thinkers across entire disciplines, including

FEMINISM, GENDER AND QUEER STUDIES

Simone De Beauvoir's
The Second Sex

Michel Foucault's
History of Sexuality

Betty Friedan's
The Feminine Mystique

Saba Mahmood's
*The Politics of Piety:
The Islamic Revival and
the Feminist Subject*

Joan Wallach Scott's
*Gender and the
Politics of History*

Mary Wollstonecraft's
*A Vindication of the
Rights of Woman*

Virginia Woolf's
A Room of One's Own

Judith Butler's
Gender Trouble

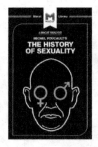

Macat analyses are available from all good bookshops and libraries.

Access hundreds of analyses through one, multimedia tool.
Join free for one month **library.macat.com**

Macat Disciplines

Access the greatest ideas and thinkers across entire disciplines, including

CRIMINOLOGY

Michelle Alexander's
*The New Jim Crow:
Mass Incarceration in the
Age of Colorblindness*

**Michael R. Gottfredson
& Travis Hirschi's**
A General Theory of Crime

Elizabeth Loftus's
Eyewitness Testimony

**Richard Herrnstein
& Charles A. Murray's**
*The Bell Curve: Intelligence and
Class Structure in American Life*

Jay Macleod's
*Ain't No Makin' It:
Aspirations and Attainment in a
Low-Income Neighborhood*

Philip Zimbardo's
The Lucifer Effect

Macat analyses are available from all good bookshops and libraries.

Access hundreds of analyses through one, multimedia tool.
Join free for one month **library.macat.com**

Macat Disciplines

Access the greatest ideas and thinkers across entire disciplines, including

INEQUALITY

Ha-Joon Chang's, *Kicking Away the Ladder*

David Graeber's, *Debt: The First 5000 Years*

Robert E. Lucas's, *Why Doesn't Capital Flow from Rich To Poor Countries?*

Thomas Piketty's, *Capital in the Twenty-First Century*

Amartya Sen's, *Inequality Re-Examined*

Mahbub Ul Haq's, *Reflections on Human Development*

Macat analyses are available from all good bookshops and libraries.

Access hundreds of analyses through one, multimedia tool.
Join free for one month **library.macat.com**

Macat Disciplines

Access the greatest ideas and thinkers across entire disciplines, including

GLOBALIZATION

Arjun Appadurai's, *Modernity at Large: Cultural Dimensions of Globalisation*

James Ferguson's, *The Anti-Politics Machine*

Geert Hofstede's, *Culture's Consequences*

Amartya Sen's, *Development as Freedom*

Macat analyses are available from all good bookshops and libraries.

Access hundreds of analyses through one, multimedia tool.
Join free for one month **library.macat.com**

Macat Disciplines

Access the greatest ideas and thinkers across entire disciplines, including

MAN AND THE ENVIRONMENT

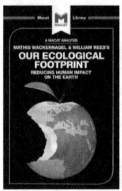

The Brundtland Report's, *Our Common Future*

Rachel Carson's, *Silent Spring*

James Lovelock's, *Gaia: A New Look at Life on Earth*

Mathis Wackernagel & William Rees's, *Our Ecological Footprint*

Macat analyses are available from all good bookshops and libraries.

Access hundreds of analyses through one, multimedia tool.
Join free for one month **library.macat.com**

Macat Disciplines

Access the greatest ideas and thinkers across entire disciplines, including

THE FUTURE OF DEMOCRACY

Robert A. Dahl's, *Democracy and Its Critics*
Robert A. Dahl's, *Who Governs?*
Alexis De Toqueville's, *Democracy in America*
Niccolò Machiavelli's, *The Prince*
John Stuart Mill's, *On Liberty*
Robert D. Putnam's, *Bowling Alone*
Jean-Jacques Rousseau's, *The Social Contract*
Henry David Thoreau's, *Civil Disobedience*

Macat analyses are available from all good bookshops and libraries.

Access hundreds of analyses through one, multimedia tool.
Join free for one month **library.macat.com**

Macat Disciplines

Access the greatest ideas and thinkers across entire disciplines, including

TOTALITARIANISM

Sheila Fitzpatrick's, *Everyday Stalinism*
Ian Kershaw's, *The "Hitler Myth"*
Timothy Snyder's, *Bloodlands*

Macat analyses are available from all good bookshops and libraries.

Access hundreds of analyses through one, multimedia tool.
Join free for one month **library.macat.com**

Macat Pairs

Analyse historical and modern issues from opposite sides of an argument. Pairs include:

RACE AND IDENTITY

Zora Neale Hurston's
Characteristics of Negro Expression

Using material collected on anthropological expeditions to the South, Zora Neale Hurston explains how expression in African American culture in the early twentieth century departs from the art of white America. At the time, African American art was often criticized for copying white culture. For Hurston, this criticism misunderstood how art works. European tradition views art as something fixed. But Hurston describes a creative process that is alive, ever-changing, and largely improvisational. She maintains that African American art works through a process called 'mimicry'—where an imitated object or verbal pattern, for example, is reshaped and altered until it becomes something new, novel—and worthy of attention.

Frantz Fanon's
Black Skin, White Masks

Black Skin, White Masks offers a radical analysis of the psychological effects of colonization on the colonized.

Fanon witnessed the effects of colonization first hand both in his birthplace, Martinique, and again later in life when he worked as a psychiatrist in another French colony, Algeria. His text is uncompromising in form and argument. He dissects the dehumanizing effects of colonialism, arguing that it destroys the native sense of identity, forcing people to adapt to an alien set of values—including a core belief that they are inferior. This results in deep psychological trauma.

Fanon's work played a pivotal role in the civil rights movements of the 1960s.

Macat analyses are available from all good bookshops and libraries.

Access hundreds of analyses through one, multimedia tool.
Join free for one month **library.macat.com**

Macat Pairs

Analyse historical and modern issues from opposite sides of an argument. Pairs include:

INTERNATIONAL RELATIONS IN THE 21ST CENTURY

Samuel P. Huntington's
The Clash of Civilisations

In his highly influential 1996 book, Huntington offers a vision of a post-Cold War world in which conflict takes place not between competing ideologies but between cultures. The worst clash, he argues, will be between the Islamic world and the West: the West's arrogance and belief that its culture is a "gift" to the world will come into conflict with Islam's obstinacy and concern that its culture is under attack from a morally decadent "other."

Clash inspired much debate between different political schools of thought. But its greatest impact came in helping define American foreign policy in the wake of the 2001 terrorist attacks in New York and Washington.

Francis Fukuyama's
The End of History and the Last Man

Published in 1992, *The End of History and the Last Man* argues that capitalist democracy is the final destination for all societies. Fukuyama believed democracy triumphed during the Cold War because it lacks the "fundamental contradictions" inherent in communism and satisfies our yearning for freedom and equality. Democracy therefore marks the endpoint in the evolution of ideology, and so the "end of history." There will still be "events," but no fundamental change in ideology.

Macat analyses are available from all good bookshops and libraries.

Access hundreds of analyses through one, multimedia tool.
Join free for one month **library.macat.com**

Macat Pairs

Analyse historical and modern issues from opposite sides of an argument. Pairs include:

HOW TO RUN AN ECONOMY

John Maynard Keynes's
The General Theory OF Employment, Interest and Money

Classical economics suggests that market economies are self-correcting in times of recession or depression, and tend toward full employment and output. But English economist John Maynard Keynes disagrees.

In his ground-breaking 1936 study *The General Theory*, Keynes argues that traditional economics has misunderstood the causes of unemployment. Employment is not determined by the price of labor; it is directly linked to demand. Keynes believes market economies are by nature unstable, and so require government intervention. Spurred on by the social catastrophe of the Great Depression of the 1930s, he sets out to revolutionize the way the world thinks

Milton Friedman's
The Role of Monetary Policy

Friedman's 1968 paper changed the course of economic theory. In just 17 pages, he demolished existing theory and outlined an effective alternate monetary policy designed to secure 'high employment, stable prices and rapid growth.'

Friedman demonstrated that monetary policy plays a vital role in broader economic stability and argued that economists got their monetary policy wrong in the 1950s and 1960s by misunderstanding the relationship between inflation and unemployment. Previous generations of economists had believed that governments could permanently decrease unemployment by permitting inflation—and vice versa. Friedman's most original contribution was to show that this supposed trade-off is an illusion that only works in the short term.

Macat analyses are available from all good bookshops and libraries.

Access hundreds of analyses through one, multimedia tool.
Join free for one month **library.macat.com**

Macat Pairs

Analyse historical and modern issues from opposite sides of an argument. Pairs include:

ARE WE FUNDAMENTALLY GOOD - OR BAD?

Steven Pinker's
The Better Angels of Our Nature

Stephen Pinker's gloriously optimistic 2011 book argues that, despite humanity's biological tendency toward violence, we are, in fact, less violent today than ever before. To prove his case, Pinker lays out pages of detailed statistical evidence. For him, much of the credit for the decline goes to the eighteenth-century Enlightenment movement, whose ideas of liberty, tolerance, and respect for the value of human life filtered down through society and affected how people thought. That psychological change led to behavioral change—and overall we became more peaceful. Critics countered that humanity could never overcome the biological urge toward violence; others argued that Pinker's statistics were flawed.

Philip Zimbardo's
The Lucifer Effect

Some psychologists believe those who commit cruelty are innately evil. Zimbardo disagrees. In *The Lucifer Effect*, he argues that sometimes good people do evil things simply because of the situations they find themselves in, citing many historical examples to illustrate his point. Zimbardo details his 1971 Stanford prison experiment, where ordinary volunteers playing guards in a mock prison rapidly became abusive. But he also describes the tortures committed by US army personnel in Iraq's Abu Ghraib prison in 2003—and how he himself testified in defence of one of those guards. committed by US army personnel in Iraq's Abu Ghraib prison in 2003—and how he himself testified in defence of one of those guards.

Macat analyses are available from all good bookshops and libraries.

Access hundreds of analyses through one, multimedia tool.
Join free for one month **library.macat.com**

Macat Pairs

Analyse historical and modern issues from opposite sides of an argument. Pairs include:

HOW WE RELATE TO EACH OTHER AND SOCIETY

Jean-Jacques Rousseau's
The Social Contract

Rousseau's famous work sets out the radical concept of the 'social contract': a give-and-take relationship between individual freedom and social order.

If people are free to do as they like, governed only by their own sense of justice, they are also vulnerable to chaos and violence. To avoid this, Rousseau proposes, they should agree to give up some freedom to benefit from the protection of social and political organization. But this deal is only just if societies are led by the collective needs and desires of the people, and able to control the private interests of individuals. For Rousseau, the only legitimate form of government is rule by the people.

Robert D. Putnam's
Bowling Alone

In *Bowling Alone*, Robert Putnam argues that Americans have become disconnected from one another and from the institutions of their common life, and investigates the consequences of this change.

Looking at a range of indicators, from membership in formal organizations to the number of invitations being extended to informal dinner parties, Putnam demonstrates that Americans are interacting less and creating less "social capital" – with potentially disastrous implications for their society.

It would be difficult to overstate the impact of *Bowling Alone*, one of the most frequently cited social science publications of the last half-century.

Macat analyses are available from all good bookshops and libraries.

Access hundreds of analyses through one, multimedia tool.
Join free for one month **library.macat.com**

Printed in the United States
by Baker & Taylor Publisher Services